Munich

Text: Jack Altman
Updated by: Trudie Trox
Managing Editor: Tony Halliday

Berlitz POCKET GUIDE

Munich

Fifth Edition 2005
Updated 2007

PHOTOGRAPHY CREDITS
AKG 22, 23, 24; Bavarian Tourist Board 100; demetrio Carrasco/JAI/Corbis 80; Chris Coe 6, 8, 15, 17, 32, 43, 49, 51, 53, 60, 71, 75, 77, 81; Bildagentur Huber/ R. Schmid 76; Tony Halliday 7, 10, 11, 18, 20, 28, 30, 35, 37, 50, 54, 62, 64, 66–7, 69, 87, 89, 94, 97; Kulturzentrum am Gasteig 68, 82; Kunstareal München 58, 59, 61; Gerd Pfeiffer 13; Marton Radkai 72; Phil Wood 12, 33, 36, 38, 40, 42, 44, 46, 56, 73, 78, 84, 85, 86, 91, 93, 99

CONTACTING THE EDITORS
Every effort has been made to provide accurate information in this publication, but changes are inevitable. The publisher cannot be responsible for any resulting loss, inconvenience or injury. We would appreciate it if readers would call our attention to any errors or outdated information by contacting Berlitz Publishing, PO Box 7910, London SE1 1WE, England. Fax: (44) 20 7403 0290; e-mail: berlitz@apaguide.co.uk www.berlitzpublishing.com

Alter Peter (page 35), Munich's oldest church, providing great views of the city and the Alps

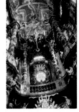
Asamkirche (page 41), a theatrical masterpiece of sculpture, decoration and light, created by the brothers Asam

Marienplatz (page 31), Munich's main square with the Column of the Virgin Mary at its centre

TOP TEN ATTRACTIONS

Stadtmuseum (page 40), providing a fascinating overview of the city's development

Olympiapark (page 75), created for the 1972 Olympic games and still a great sport and recreation area

Neuschwanstein Castle (page 76), Ludwig II's extraordinary romanticised version of the medieval world

Pinakothek der Moderne (page 60), the largest museum of art and design in Europe

Englischer Garten (page 64), featuring the Chinese Tower and its beer garden

Residenz (page 45), the fomer royal palace, with seven courtyards and this magnificent Renaissance hall, the Antiquarium

Deutsches Museum (page 68), Munich's world-class museum of science and technology

CONTENTS

THE CITY AND ITS PEOPLE

With its relaxed lifestyle, Munich seems almost Mediterranean. For many European travellers, this last main stop before the Alps provides a first breath of Italy. Munich, the capital of Bavaria, is more baroque than Gothic and more green than grey.

The city's genius has always been its ability to combine the Germanic talent for getting things done with a specifically Bavarian need to do them pleasantly. Business lunches seem to last a little longer here, and office hours seem to be a little shorter. Yet no one who has witnessed the city's impressive affluence, its dynamic car industry and its splendid underground railway system would suggest that this delightfully relaxed attitude was unproductive.

Getting around by tram

Munich is Germany's most popular tourist destination. According to opinion polls, it's also the city that Germans would most like to live in. It is not just the elegance and prosperity of the place that makes it such a magnet, but the vivacious way of life which is best savoured in one of its many beer gardens, beer cellars or just out and about on the town, particularly during the long and usually very hot and balmy summers. As the capital of the Catholic and conservative Free State of Bavaria, Munich epitomises the independent Bavarian spirit. But it is also a highly cosmopolitan city, where people from all over the world can and do feel at home.

Munich is also home to the raucous Oktoberfest, and it is, perhaps, this single event that first strikes the popular imagination in relation to the city. Indeed, with annual consumption of 6 million litres of beer by 6.5 million visitors, it is a grandiose event, quite appropriate to the oversized image the Bavarians have of their capital. It is also the most extravagant expression of that untranslatable feeling of warm fellowship known in German as *Gemütlichkeit*.

Cultural Centre

But it would be wrong to think of life in Munich merely as one long Oktoberfest. As a result of the post-war division of Berlin, Munich became the undisputed cultural capital of the Federal Republic of Germany – no mean achievement, in the face of the considerable claims of Hamburg and Cologne. The opera house and concert halls make the town a musical mecca still,

Gemütlichkeit in a beer garden

especially for the performance of works by Richard Strauß, Mozart and Wagner. Wagner's patron was 'mad' King Ludwig II of Bavaria, who was responsible for the 'fairytale' Neuschwanstein Castle in the Alpine foothills, but it was his grandfather, Ludwig I, who established the city's cultural credentials by assembling vast collections and building places to store them in. That legacy lives on in Munich, and the city is endowed with some

Munich is the capital of Bavaria and of the administrative district of Upper Bavaria. It lies on a plain to the north of the Alpine foothills, about 530m (1,700ft) above sea level. The population of the city, which covers about 310 sq km (120 sq miles), is around 1.35 million, making the Bavarian metropolis the third-largest city in Germany, trailing only Berlin and Hamburg.

fabulous art collections, from the Old Masters in the Alte Pinakothek to the main avant-garde movements represented in the Pinakothek der Moderne. Painters have long appreciated the favourable artistic climate of the city, particularly in the bohemian district of Schwabing, which exploded onto the international scene in the early 20th century as a centre for the Blaue Reiter school, whose ranks included Wassily Kandinsky, Paul Klee and Franz Marc.

Munich has become a centre for industry and publishing, and also for the much-admired New German Cinema and its world-famous directors, Volker Schloendorff, Werner Herzog and Edgar Reitz.

But there is also a darker side to the city, including Adolf Hitler's early association with Munich and the formation here of the Nazi Party. The stormy years from 1918 to 1945 were, in the end, a brief political interlude for the city, and its people seem happy to have relinquished the political spotlight to Bonn and Berlin.

Elegant Ludwigstraße

Restored Heritage

Munich has tried, however, to retain its historical identity.
After the destruction resulting from World War II, many
German cities decided to break with the past and rebuild in
a completely modern style. But the Bavarian capital preferred to painstakingly restore and reconstruct the great
churches and palaces of its past. There are plenty of modern office buildings on the periphery, but the heart of the
old city has successfully recaptured its rich architectural
heritage and charm. There are still some reminders of the
ravages of war, and monuments such as the Siegestor (Victory Gate, in Ludwigstraße) have been left in their bomb-
scarred condition as a history lesson.

The inner city is a pedestrian's delight, thanks both to a
clever road system that keeps the majority of the traffic
circling the city centre rather than crossing through it (except
by means of underpasses) and to an excellent system of

public transport. Beyond the city centre the broad, tree-lined avenues and boulevards planned by Bavaria's last kings open up the town and provide a considerable touch of elegance.

Open Spaces

The Englischer Garten, immensely enhanced by the ebullient River Isar, is a real jewel among Europe's great parks. The river's swiftly flowing waters are evidence of the proximity of the Alps, where the river has its source. On a clear day, the mountains seem to lie just beyond the city's southern suburbs. That's when the *Föhn* is blowing; this famous southerly wind gives some people a headache and inspires others with phenomenally clear creative insights – a characteristic Munich ambiguity.

When the mountains appear on the city's doorstep, locals are reminded of the countryside from which many of them, or their parents, originated. Every weekend there is a mass exodus to the surrounding villages and lakes: east to the Chiemsee; west and south to the Ammersee, Starnberger See and Tegernsee. In the winter, they trek farther south into the mountains for skiing, an integral part of Munich life, which most kids begin learning almost as soon as they can walk.

The River Isar with the Volksbad

Although Munich is undoubtedly a metropolis, and in many ways a sophisticated one, the city also retains a resolutely rural atmosphere, never losing sight of its origins in the hinterland. Visitors can easily participate in Munich's happy mixture of town and country.

A BRIEF HISTORY

Munich was a relatively late arrival on the Bavarian scene. During the Middle Ages, at a time when Nuremberg, Augsburg and Regensburg were already thriving cities, the present-day state capital was no more than a small settlement housing a few peasants and some Benedictine monks from Tegernsee. The site was known in the 8th century quite simply as *Ze den Munichen,* a dialect form of *zu den Mönchen* ('the monks' place'). Accordingly, Munich's coat of arms today bears the image of a child in a monk's habit, the Münchner Kindl.

In 1158, the settlement of the River Isar attracted the attention of Heinrich der Löwe (Henry the Lion), the Duke of Saxony and Bavaria, who was cousin of the German Emperor Frederick Barbarossa. He was looking for a place to set up a toll station for the passage of salt, a lucrative product from nearby Salzburg. Until then, tolls had been collected by the powerful bishop of Freising at Oberföhring Bridge, just to the north. Duke Heinrich burned this bridge down and built a new one, together with a market, customs house and mint, at a fork in the Isar.

The Münchner Kindl

Bishop Otto of Freising was an uncle of Frederick Barbarossa, and protested to the emperor, who decided to leave Munich in Heinrich's hands, but to grant one-third of the toll revenues to the diocese of Freising – dues that were paid until 1852. The day of the emperor's decision, 14 June 1158, is recognised as the date of Munich's founding.

The salt trade made Munich prosperous, and the settlement grew rapidly into a town. In 1180, after Heinrich refused military aid for the emperor's foreign wars, Frederick Barbarossa threatened to raze Munich to the ground. However, Bishop Otto pleaded the city's case, as he was making a great deal of money from his share of the salt duty. Munich was saved, but the city was handed over to the Wittelsbach family, who ruled Bavaria for the next seven centuries.

Ludwig the Bavarian

The Wittelsbachs Take Over

By the end of the 13th century, Munich was the largest town in the Wittelsbach dominions. However, the prosperous Munich burghers grew discontented and began to press Duke Ludwig the Stern (1229–94) for a larger piece of the pie. In defence, the duke built himself a fortress, the Alter Hof, parts of which can still be seen just northeast of Marienplatz.

Munich entered the international political arena in 1328, when Duke Ludwig IV (1294–1347) was made Holy Roman Emperor. With his court firmly established in Munich, he enlisted scholars from all over Europe as his advisors. Perhaps the most notable of these were Marsiglio of Padua

William of Occam became famous for 'Occam's Razor', in which he states, roughly, that if you've found a simple explanation for a problem, don't look for a complicated one. The Bavarians like that kind of thinking.

and William of Occam, philosophers who defended secular power against that of the Pope and thus made themselves useful allies for Ludwig.

Troubled Times

The Black Death brought devastation to Munich in 1348. The city suffered social unrest, abrupt economic decline and the debasement of its currency. In an irrational reaction to the catastrophe, citizens went on a wild rampage, massacring Jews for alleged ritual murder.

High taxes and widespread penury caused the burghers to revolt against the patricians. In 1385, the people took a cloth merchant, Hans Impler, from his house to the Schrannenplatz (now Marienplatz) and beheaded him. The patricians and their princes demanded financial compensation, and the situation deteriorated into open rebellion from 1397 to 1403.

By bringing in heavy military reinforcements, the Wittelsbachs regained the upper hand without being forced to make any of the far-reaching civic concessions won by the guilds of other German towns such as Augsburg, Hamburg and Cologne. To secure their position during these troubled times, the Wittelsbachs built a sturdy Residenz on what was then the northwest corner of town. The massive, fortress-like palace *(see page 45)* attests to the level of protection needed to keep this despotic monarchy safe from its own people.

Reform and Counter-Reform

Dissent eased in the 15th century, and trade boomed in salt, wine and cloth. The town also served as a transit point for the rich 'Venice goods' of spices and gold. The great Frauenkirche, still a town symbol, as well as the Gothic civic citadel of the Altes Rathaus, were built during this period of renewed prosperity.

By the middle of the 16th century, an architectural rivalry had grown up between the burghers, who favoured the German Gothic style for their homes, and the Bavarian nobles, who preferred the Renaissance styles of Spain and Italy. The appearance of Munich in the 1500s is preserved in Jakob Sandtner's city model on display in the Bavarian National Museum. However, most of the original buildings were later replaced by the baroque and rococo palaces of the 17th and 18th centuries and the neo-Gothic and neo-classical buildings of the Industrial Revolution.

The Frauenkirche

The Bavarian aristocracy's preference for foreign styles was in many ways a reaction to the subversive implications of German nationalism, which had grown out of the Reformation. In 1510, when Martin Luther passed through Munich on his way to Rome, his still relatively orthodox preaching met with sympathy. But some 10 years later Luther's revolutionary position aroused the anger of the traditionally conservative Bavarians, and Duke Wilhelm IV introduced the severe measures advocated by the Jesuits. Rebellious monks and priests were arrested and executed. In 1527, the repression culminated in the drowning or burning of 29 members of Munich's Baptist community who refused to recant.

The religious conflict concealed a competition for political and economic power. The city's bourgeoisie had seen in the Reformation an opportunity to push for the social reforms which the aristocracy had adamantly resisted. In the struggles that followed, the burghers were forced to relinquish the salt monopoly to the administration of the state.

With a certain vindictiveness, the nobles flaunted their political triumph with sumptuous festivities at court, such as those arranged to pay homage to Emperor Charles V and his Spanish retinue during their Munich visit of 1530. The climax of such pomp and circumstance in grand Renaissance style was the three-week-long wedding celebration of Duke Wilhelm V and his bride, Renata of Lorraine, in 1568.

The patricians received much spiritual support from the Jesuits, who were brought to Munich by Duke Wilhelm V to establish a school and to set up a theatre for the performance of morality plays. Some people resented this influence, laying the foundation for the now perennial Bavarian distrust of outsiders.

Good Money After Bad

Such extravagant expenditure meant that the state coffers were empty by the time Maximilian I (1573–1651) came to the throne. Even though the Bavarian state was now almost completely bankrupt, Maximilian (who was made Prince Elector in 1623) proceeded to build up a magnificent collection of art works. However painful this may have been for his tax-crippled subjects, we can be thankful to him for having thus laid the foundations of the Alte Pinakothek.

It was also Maximilian who ordered the splendid decorations that embellish the Residenz. Gustavus Adolphus of Sweden, who invaded Munich in 1632 during the cruel Thirty Years' War, was so impressed with the Residenz that he said he would have liked to carry the whole thing back to Stockholm on wheels. Instead, he settled for 42 Munich citizens, who were taken hostage against payment by Bavaria of 300,000 Thaler in war reparations. (All but six of them returned three years later.)

In the Thirty Years' War (1618–48), bombardment damage was less in Munich than in many other German towns. However, starvation and disease wrought more havoc than the cannon. In 1634 the Black Death struck, killing 7,000 inhabitants – a third of the city's population. In 1638, Maximilian set up the Mariensäule (Column of the Virgin Mary) as thanks for the town's deliverance from suffering.

The Antiquarium in the Residenz, built around 1570

Munich's Prince Electors frequently involved the city in costly foreign adventures, thus rubbing salt into the wounds of civic poverty. In 1683, Maximilian II Emanuel decided to help the Austrians beat off the Turks besieging Vienna. He promptly set out for Belgrade, and returned bringing 296 Turks as sedan-chair bearers and road-builders — Munich's first *Gastarbeiter* (immigrant workers). The Turkish Wars are commemorated in huge paintings that are on display in Schleißheim Castle. The city was saddled with an immense debt as a result of the war.

During the War of the Spanish Succession (1701–14) Maximilian II Emanuel fought, along with the French, on the

Archbishop's Palace

losing side and Munich had to bear the unfortunate burden of Austrian occupation from 1704 to 1714. When the farmers rebelled in 1705, the ringleaders were arrested and hanged, drawn and quartered on Marienplatz. Their heads were displayed on pikes at Isartor (Isar Gate).

After the war, the Bavarian aristocracy was not especially sympathetic to the tribulations of the citizenry. The nobles set about building splendid little palaces for themselves, including the Preysing Palais, the Archbishop's Palais and the Törring-Jettenbach Palais, strategically situated near the Prince Elector's Residenz.

Peace in an English Garden

The people of Munich grew ever more xenophobic after Hungarian hussars took over the city in 1742. They were dispatched by Empress Maria Theresa in retaliation for the Bavarian Prince Elector's opposition to Austro-Hungarian involvement in Germany.

In this atmosphere of hostility, Maximilian III Joseph (1727–77) could not have been surprised when the Munich bourgeoisie resisted his efforts to establish a court monopoly on the manufacture of goods. All the royal manufacturers went bankrupt, with the exception of Nymphenburg porcelain, which thrives to this day. A brighter note was struck with the building of the delightful Cuvilliés-Theater and the performance there by one Wolfgang Amadeus Mozart of his operas *Idomeneo* (premiered there in 1781), *The Abduction from the Seraglio*, *The Marriage of Figaro* and *The Magic Flute*.

When Maximilian III Joseph, the last of the true Wittelsbach line, died in 1777, the succession fell to Karl Theodor, a member of the Mannheim branch of the family. He didn't want to leave Mannheim, he didn't like Munich and Munich didn't like him. The people were starving. Instead of bread, Karl Theodor sent in soldiers to suppress the angry populace.

It was Benjamin Thompson, an American, who suggested a solution to Karl Theodor's predicament. With the prince's blessing, Count Rumford (as he was subsequently known) provided schools and work to keep the unruly soldiers off the streets. He set up workshops and soup kitchens for the poor. (The potato-and-barley soup that was dispensed in them, served in Munich to this day, is known as *Rumfordsuppe*.) In 1789, Rumford requisitioned a marshy wilderness on the outskirts of town and detailed the soldiers to drain it for development as a gigantic public park. The final result of Rumford's efforts, the Englischer Garten, is an enduring monument to American enterprise.

Statue of Ludwig I

Hopes and Dreams

While Munich was cultivating its garden, the rest of Europe was in a revolutionary uproar. The city could not remain isolated for long. In 1800 it was occupied by the French troops of General Jean Victor Moreau, who established his headquarters in Nymphenburg Palace.

Napoleon himself came to town in 1805 for the marriage of his wife Josephine's son, Eugène de Beauharnais, to Princess Augusta of Bavaria. The journey to Munich did not inconvenience the emperor too much, as it was on the way to Austerlitz, where he was to fight the Russians and Austrians. Napoleon elevated Maximilian IV Joseph from Prince Elector to King of Bavaria, and in exchange took a vast contingent of Bavarians on his Russian campaign of 1812, where he left 30,000 of them to die on the battlefield. Under pressure from the French, Maximilian emancipated the Protestants of Munich, improved conditions for the Jews and introduced a more moderate constitution.

Somehow, amid all the troubles of war and revolution, Munich managed to celebrate once again. Heeding the new spirit of the times, the royal court chose not to exclude the populace from the celebrations in honour of the marriage of Maximilian's son, Ludwig, to Theresa of Saxony. On 17 October 1810, horseraces were organised, with great success. They developed into an annual event – now the Oktoberfest.

Munich itself was gradually expanding to the north and west into Maxvorstadt, a region that links the city centre to

Schwabing. The Graeco-Roman architecture of the National-theater brought to the city the first signs of the Classical spirit that was to become the obsession of Ludwig I.

Born in Strasbourg, Ludwig (1786–1868) was determined to break the French stranglehold on German culture and to make Munich the leader of a new nationalist movement. During the Napoleonic occupation, the civic symbol of the Münchner Kindl had been replaced with an imperial lion; Ludwig made sure that the little monk was restored.

Familiar with the architecture of Rome and the Greek monuments of Sicily, Ludwig wanted to turn Munich into an 'Athens-on-the-Isar'. His first step was to move Bavaria's university from Landshut to Munich, where it was established along Ludwigstraße in the Maxvorstadt area first developed under his father's rule.

Königsplatz, with its Greek Revival architecture, was the most complete realisation of Ludwig's Classical aspirations. Typically, Ludwig himself laid the foundation stone for the Alte Pinakothek (the gallery designed to house the royal art

Her Name Was Lola

A prodigious worker, rising before dawn each day to go to his office in the Residenz, Ludwig I gained some diversion from his sober duties by commissioning a series of portraits of the most beautiful young women of Munich. The collection hangs in the Schönheitsgalerie (Gallery of Beautiful Women) at the Nymphenburg Palace. Included is his mistress, a dancer known as Lola Montez, with whom he fell in love when he was 60 and she 28. She was Ludwig's ruin. He made her the Countess von Landsfeld, to the horror both of his conservative ministers and the radical university students.

In 1848, as revolution swept Europe, the students and angry citizens of Munich forced Ludwig to deport Lola, and he abdicated in disgust.

collections) on 7 April 1826, the anniversary of the painter Raphael's birth. Ludwig's successor Maximilian II (1811–64) boosted Munich's cultural reputation thanks to his intimacy with illustrious thinkers such as the historian Leopold von Ranke, the philosopher Friedrich von Schelling and the chemist Justus von Liebig.

End of a Dream

The last great king of Bavaria was the romantic king Ludwig II (1845–86), famous for his collaboration with Richard Wagner. Under Ludwig's patronage, the composer staged in Munich the premières of his operas *Tristan und Isolde*, *Die Meistersinger von Nürnberg*, *Das Rheingold* and *Die Walküre*.

In the mundane world of 19th-century industrial expansion, Ludwig dreamt of making Munich the music capital of the world. He wanted to build a gigantic theatre for his idol Wagner, a place where the composer could develop his concept of *Gesamtkunstwerk* – a synthesis of music, lyrics and theatre. But the banalities of state finances interfered and he was forced to relinquish the project to Bayreuth.

Ludwig acted out his fantasies in the eccentric fairytale

Living the dream: Ludwig II

palaces he built outside Munich – a medieval castle at Neuschwanstein, a beautiful French château at Linderhof and a fanciful version of Versailles' Grand Trianon at Herrenchiemsee. Ironically, it was at a castle (the 16th-century Schloss Berg on Lake Starnberg) that Ludwig's life came to a sad and mysterious end. By 1886, his wild behaviour had per-

Der Blaue Reiter by Wassily Kandinsky

suaded the Bavarian government that he was mad, and a special commission declared him to be so. In consequence, the
director of a mental asylum accompanied him to Schloss
Berg and the two were later found drowned. It has never
been determined whether their deaths were the result of murder or suicide.

Uncle Luitpold took over as regent (in place of Ludwig's
brother, the insane King Otto). He presided over the grand
fin de siècle artistic movement of the *Jugendstil*. This was
followed a generation later by the *Blaue Reiter* (Blue Rider)
school, which included Wassily Kandinsky, Paul Klee, Franz
Marc and Gabriele Münter. Thomas Mann, Rainer Maria
Rilke, Stefan George and other writers moved to Schwabing.
The artistic ferment also attracted a young painter from Vienna, an embittered man named Adolf Hitler.

The Wittelsbach dynasty, along with others in Vienna and
Berlin, ended in the disaster of World War I. Bavarians

Marching for the Bavarian Republic in 1919

resented having been dragged into the European conflict by what they felt was Prussian belligerence, and a new social democratic movement gained support. In November 1918, with the war in its last days, Kurt Eisner led a march of workers and peasants from the Theresienwiese. En route, disaffected soldiers took control of their barracks and hoisted the red flag of revolution. The Bavarian Republic was declared in the Mathäser Bräuhaus (breweries traditionally being a favoured spot for political action in Munich). The people invaded the Residenz and wandered around hooting for echoes in the vast galleries and ballrooms. Ludwig III, the last Wittelsbach king, fled in a car from the palace.

But the newly born republic of workers, peasants and soldiers, modelled on the Soviets created under the Russian revolution, was subject to violent attack from the conservative press and from private armies of troops *(Freikorps)* roaming the streets. Playing on Bavarian xenophobia, the right wing attacked Eisner as a Berliner and as a Jew. Just three months after the November revolution, Eisner was dead, shot down by a young aristocrat hoping to curry favour with an extreme right-wing club.

A group of 'coffee-house anarchists' led by the writers Ernst Toller and Erich Mühsam took over briefly, but they were soon replaced by hard-line communists. After fierce and bloody fighting with the Freikorps, the Bavarian Red Army was defeated, and the short-lived independent republic of Bavaria was crushed.

In the space of six months, Munich had known in breathtaking succession a monarchy, revolutionary socialism, moderate socialism, anarchy, communism and, finally, brutal counter-revolutionary oppression. Thus, a tolerant tradition was swept away and the city became a breeding ground for extremist political and paramilitary groups.

Hitler's Munich

Adolf Hitler had first been drawn to Munich by its cultural ambience, but he remained immune to the innovative tendencies of the avant-garde. His own painting was stolidly academic and attracted no attention. He turned to the clamour of German nationalism, and a chance photograph taken at a rally on Odeonsplatz in August 1914 shows Hitler in the crowd, joyfully greeting news of the declaration of war.

He returned to Munich as a corporal in 1918. It was while working to re-educate soldiers in nationalistic, anti-Marxist ideas at the end of the Bavarian Republic that he joined the Deutsche Arbeiter-Partei. By February 1920, he was able to address 2,000 members in the Hofbräuhaus. The association soon became known as the Nationalsozialistische Deutsche Arbeiter-Partei, or Nazi Party. Its symbol was the swastika. Armed storm troops of the party's Sturm-Abteilung (SA) broke up any opposition political meetings held in Munich.

At a January 1923 meeting, Hitler said: 'Either the Nazi Party is the German movement of the future, in which case no devil can stop it, or it isn't, in which case it deserves to be destroyed'. Both proved true. By November, the party had 55,000 members and 15,000 storm troops. Hitler then felt strong enough to stage his famous Beer Hall Putsch.

This was intended as a first move in the campaign to force the Bavarian state government to cooperate in a Nazi march on Berlin. The putsch ended in a debacle on Odeonsplatz with Hitler being sent to prison, but not before he had turned the whole affair to his advantage. He ensured that his trial for treason became an indictment of his prosecutors as accomplices of the 'November criminals' who, he said, had stabbed Germany in the back in 1918 with their anti-war movement. Hitler became an instant hero. In prison at nearby Landsberg, he was was not required to perform prison duties, but instead held political meetings and used his time to write his manifesto, *Mein Kampf.*

Beer, Bluff and Bullets

The Beer Hall Putsch, which launched Hitler's national career, was staged in the Bürgerbräukeller. It gave a foretaste of the crazy melodrama, bluff and shameless gall he was later to exhibit on the world scene.

With the Bavarian minister Gustav von Kahr about to speak, Hitler burst into the crowded room, smashed a beer mug to the floor, and pushed forward at the head of his storm troops, brandishing a pistol. In the pandemonium, he jumped on a table and fired a shot into the ceiling. 'National revolution has broken out!' he yelled. 'Farce! South America!' was the response from a few wags, who were promptly beaten up. The new Hitler style of politics had indisputably arrived. Today the Bürgerbräukeller has been replaced by the Hilton City Hotel; there is no plaque commemorating the putsch.

Hitler's career took him to Berlin, but the Nazis kept their party headquarters in Munich at the Brown House (named after the colour of their shirts). Brighter spirits of the time, including the whimsical comedian Karl Valentin and a fan of his, the dramatist Bertolt Brecht, also made their home in Munich.

Resistance leaders Hans and Sophie Scholl

In 1935, Munich became known as the 'Capital of the (Nazi) Movement'. Its status at the vanguard was confirmed in June 1938, when the central synagogue was looted, presaging the *Kristallnacht* (Night of Broken Glass) rampage five months later, when most of Germany's Jewish shops and houses of prayer were destroyed.

In September of that year, Munich also became a symbol of the ignominious appeasement decisions by Britain and France. In Munich's Führerbau, a meeting took place between prime ministers Neville Chamberlain and Edouard Daladier, during which they negotiated the dismemberment of Czechoslovakia with Hitler and Mussolini. Later, Chamberlain obtained a signed piece of paper from the Führer, which he waved at the British people as a guarantee of 'peace in our time'.

War and Peace

Large-scale resistance to the Nazis was not possible in wartime Munich, but there were voices of dissent. They included the *Weiße Rose* (White Rose) student movement, which courageously distributed anti-Hitler leaflets at the university. But the protagonists were soon found out, and the founders, Hans and Sophie Scholl and Christoph Probst, were guillotined on 22 February 1943; other leading members met the same gruesome end two months later.

World War II brought 71 air raids to the city, killing 6,000 and wounding 16,000. Bombardments were most intense in 1944, heavily damaging the Frauenkirche, St Peter's and St Michael's churches, as well as large parts of the Residenz and Alte Pinakothek. The Brown House was destroyed but, ironically, the majority of Hitler's other buildings were left intact.

The postwar reconstruction was a triumph of hard work and fiercely loyal attachment to the great traditions of Munich's past. Monuments, palaces and churches were all restored with meticulous care. Traditionally open to the arts and to good living in general, Munich expanded and became Germany's third-largest city (total population 1.35 million), welcoming many Berliners and refugees from the former eastern territories.

Friedensengel (Angel of Peace)

The city has continued to build on its international reputation as a city of culture, with a year-round programme of performing-arts productions, including concerts and open-air opera in the beautiful surroundings of the great palaces and monuments. Visitors to Munich can be sure of a taste of good living, Bavarian-style.

Historical Landmarks

8th century Small settlement of Benedictine monks gives the site its name, Ze den Munichen.

1158 Henry the Lion sets up toll station for the passage of salt from Salzburg.

1180 Emperor Frederick Barbarossa takes Munich from Henry and hands the city over to the Wittelsbach family.

1328 Duke Ludwig IV becomes Holy Roman Emperor and his court is established in Munich.

1348 Black Death brings devastation to Munich.

15th century A period of prosperity – Munich established as transit point for trade from Venice.

1632 Swedish armies invade Munich during the Thirty Years' War; the city devastated by plague.

1638 Mariensäule set up on Marienplatz.

1704–1714 Austrian occupation of Munich.

1742 Hungarian hussars take over the city.

1789 American Benjamin Thompson develops the Englischer Garten.

1805 Napoleon visits Munich.

1806 Napoleon raises Bavaria to status of kingdom.

1826 Ludwig I lays the foundation stone for the Alte Pinakothek.

1845 Bavarian King Ludwig II is born.

1886 Ludwig II found drowned in Lake Starnberg close to Schloss Berg.

1918 The Bavarian Republic declared. Ludwig III flees.

1919 Kurt Eisner, leader of a short-lived socialist regime, assassinated.

1923 Adolf Hitler stages his famous 'Beer Hall Putsch'.

1935 Munich named capital of the Nazi Movement.

1939–1945 World War II: 71 air raids on the city, killing 6,000 and wounding 16,000.

1972 Munich hosts the Summer Olympic Games.

1991 Munich becomes part of a reunified Germany.

2002 Pinakothek der Moderne opened. Germany adopts the euro.

2006 Jewish Museum of Munich opened at St-Jakobs-Platz.

WHERE TO GO

Munich has two enormous assets as far as the visitor is concerned. First, a large majority of the city's museums, monuments, palaces and churches are concentrated in the Innenstadt (inner city), which makes Munich a great town for walking. Second, the superb public transport system, which incorporates buses, trams, underground (U-Bahn) and rapid district trains (S-Bahn), brings all the other sights within easy reach. There is absolutely no need for a car.

Munich long ago expanded beyond the confines of its medieval boundaries, and the old city wall has now disappeared. However, the remains of three gates survive to indicate the perimeter of the inner city – Isartor, Karlstor and Sendlinger Tor – as well as Odeonsplatz, a rendezvous for salt traders setting off in the 14th century for northern Germany. Ever since Munich's earliest beginnings, however, Marienplatz has been at the heart of it all.

IN AND AROUND MARIENPLATZ

Until the middle of the 19th century, **Marienplatz** was the place where the wheat market was held. The square was the obvious site for the town hall, and was the place where criminals were hanged. Marienplatz was also the scene of the most extravagant wedding Munich has ever seen – that of Duke Wilhelm V to Renata of Lorraine in 1568. It was the inevitable choice for the central junction of the U-Bahn and S-Bahn system in 1972.

Graced with its tubs of flowers and outdoor cafés, Marienplatz today forms part of an attractive pedestrian zone. It is the home of the **Mariensäule** (Column of the Virgin Mary),

The Neues Rathaus on Marienplatz, with the Fischbrunnen

erected in 1638 by Maximilian I in gratitude for the town's deliverance from the Plague after its defeat by the Swedes during the Thirty Years' War. At the base of the column are a basilisk, dragon, serpent and lion – which represent plague, hunger, heresy and war – each being vanquished by heroic cherubs. On the top of the monument is the gilded figure of Mary, who watches over Munich. Holding Jesus in her left arm and a sceptre in her right, she is a reminder of Munich's religious foundation. The square also contains the partially reconstructed 19th-century **Fischbrunnen** monument. Young butchers used to leap into the bronze fountain at the end of their apprenticeship, but today the tradition is kept up only by Fasching (carnival) revellers or happy soccer fans.

Two Town Halls

Standing at the eastern end of Marienplatz is the picturesque **Altes Rathaus** (Old Town Hall), an example of Munich's efforts to reconstruct, rather than replace, the remnants of its venerable history. The dove-grey facade, amber-tiled steeple and graceful little spires of this Gothic-style edifice capture the spirit of the 15th-century original designed by Jörg von Halsbach (also called Jörg Gang-

Altes Rathaus by night

hofer), though it isn't an exact replica. In any case, with the addition over the centuries of a baroque, onion-shaped cupola and then an overconscientious 'regothification', the building that was destroyed by Allied bombs was probably further from the original than what you see today. Adjacent to the main building, the fairytale clocktower provides the perfect setting for the **Spielzeug-museum** (Toy Museum, open daily 10am–5.30pm). Its fascinating collections, ranging from antique train sets to animals in the zoo, are spread over four floors linked by a spiral staircase.

The Old Town Hall contains a banqueting hall, but the daily business of city government takes place at the **Neues Rathaus** (New Town Hall) on the northern side of the square. This is a fine example of 19th-century Neo-Gothic architecture: proud and self-assertive, its facade is elaborately decorated with the statues of

The Glockenspiel

kings, princes and dukes, saints, allegorical figures and characters from the folklore of Munich. The tower is 85m (260ft) high; its main attraction, apart from the splendid view (lift to the top; open Mon–Fri, summer also weekends) is the 43-bell **Glockenspiel** (carillon) which puts on three shows daily, at 11am, noon and 5pm. Two groups of figures appear, one group re-enacting the tournament held during the wedding of Duke Wilhelm V and Renata of Lorraine and the other, underneath, recreating the cooper's dance (*Schäfflertanz*), which was performed to cheer up the surviving populace after the plague of 1517. In the evening, at 9pm, a night watchman with lantern blows his horn and an angel of peace blesses the little Munich monk (Münchner Kindl).

Frauenkirche

In addition to its twin towers, the Frauenkirche is known for its 'Devil's Footprint'. Jörg von Halsbach made a pact with the devil that in return for the money to complete the church he would design it without any visible windows. This was but an illusion, however, there being just one point near the entrance from which no windows could be seen. Thus deceived, the devil stamped his foot in fury; both imprint and illusion can be seen to this day.

Now go along Weinstraße (beginning at the west side of Marienplatz) and left along Sporerstraße to reach Frauenplatz and the enormous Domkirche zu Unserer Lieben Frau (Cathedral Church of Our Lady), usually referred to simply as the **Frauenkirche**. With its twin brick towers and their bulbous domes (99m/325ft high) dominating the centre of the city, this church has always been Munich's defining landmark. An austere, unadorned Gothic structure, it was built between 1468 and 1488 by Jörg von Halsbach (Jörg Ganghofer). The Italian Renaissance domes are an addition of 1524.

The stark interior was reconstructed from the rubble of World War II bombardments – a truly heroic work of restoration. The original Gothic windows in the choir, stored in safety during the war, give an impression of the church's former glory. Fine sculptures of the Apostles and Prophets also escaped destruction and adorn the choir as before. They were created by Erasmus Grasser *(see page 40)* in 1502. A fine altarpiece of 1483 by Friedrich Pacher, the *Baptism of Christ*, hangs in the north chapel. It is flanked by Jan Polack's panels depicting Jesus on the Mount of Olives and his arrest, crucifixion and burial. Notice, too, the 17th-century funerary monument of Emperor Ludwig the Bavarian, who died in 1347.

It's possible to ascend the **South Tower** by lift for a good view over the city (April to October Mon–Sat 10am–5pm).

Alter Peter

Looming over the south side of Marienplatz, but not quite on the square itself, is **St Peter's**, the oldest church in Munich, dating from before the foundation of the city itself in 1158, hence it's nickname Alter Peter – Old Peter. The original structure gave way to a building in the Romanesque style, succeeded in time by a Gothic church that boasted a twin-steepled tower. Everything but the tower was obliterated in the great fire of 1327, and a new Gothic structure went up. This was remodelled along Renaissance lines in the 17th century, and a new tower with a single steeple was created. Destroyed in the war, St Peter's has been faithfully reconstructed. It's well worth climbing the 306 steps to the observation balcony at the top for the **stunning views** over the city (entrance off Rindermarkt; open summer Mon–Sat 9am–6.30pm, Sun 10am–6.30pm, winter last entry 5.30pm).

The tower of the Alter Peter

The crowning piece of the light, bright interior is the **high altar** glorifying Peter and the fathers of the Church. It was restored from the remnants of the 18th-century original, inspired by Bernini's altar for St Peter's in Rome. Egid Quirin Asam *(see page 41)* was the designer of the ensemble, incorporating Erasmus Grasser's *St Peter*. The gilded wood figures of the Church fathers are the masterly work of Egid Quirin. Leading up to the altar are splendid rococo choir stalls. You'll also see five of Jan Polack's Late Gothic paintings that once adorned the altar. They show Peter healing the lame, enthroned, at sea, in prison and on the cross. Also from the Late Gothic period is the Schrenk-Altar, a fine early 15th-century sandstone relief of the Crucifixion and the Day of Judgment.

Viktualienmarkt

Just behind St Peter's, at the other side of Rosenstraße, lies one of the most colourful locations in Munich and a magnet for all who love food, the **Viktualienmarkt**. The city's central market

Viktualienmarkt grocer

has been doing business here since 1807. Stroll around the enticing stalls with their myriad cheeses and exotic spices, breads, meats, fruit and vegetables. In 2005, Munich celebrated the opening of the reconstructed **Schrannenhalle**. This 19th-century iron and glass structure was an iconic city landmark, and it now brims once again with shop life and Bavarian gastronomy 24 hours a day, 7 days a week.

The cheerful atmosphere of the market makes it the perfect place for annual performances of the Marketwomen's Dance, held on Shrove Tuesday. It's also the scene of a number of lively celebrations around the flower-bedecked maypole.

Adjacent to the market is **Heiliggeistkirche** (Church of the Holy Spirit). This 14th-century Gothic structure was extensively altered to suit the baroque tastes of the 1720s. The two styles come together perfectly in the **Marienaltar** – a lovely wooden sculpture of 1450, the *Hammerthaler Muttergottes* (Hammerthal Mother of God) originally from the Lake Tegernsee monastery,

Inside the Alter Hof

set in a gilded baroque frame. The high altar preserves a fine pair of *Adoring Angels* from 1730 by Johann Georg Greiff.

Alter Hof and the Hofbräuhaus

Coming out of the church, duck along little Burgstraße past the Altes Rathaus. Pause at No. 5 to admire the **Zum Hofer** restaurant *(see also page 138)*. One of only a handful of Gothic houses still left in Munich, this was once the home of the town clerk. Built in about 1550, it has a neatly restored leafy courtyard and a staircase tower.

Continue along Burgstraße to the **Alter Hof**, Munich's old royal residence, which was originally built in 1255 by Ludwig the Stern in the then northeastern part of the city. It was designed as a defence against foreign invaders as well as the city's own unruly burghers, but was eventually superseded by the more massive Residenz *(see page 45)*. The buildings suffered more at the hands of 19th-century urban developers than during the 20th-century bombing. However, as you pass

Symbol of the 'Royal Brewery'

through the gates into the courtyard you'll see that parts of the complex have been superbly restored. The reconstructed Burgtor (City Gate) and quaint little Affenturm (Monkey Tower) in the west wing – recapture the atmosphere of the Wittelsbachs' first Munich residence as it was in the 15th century. The heraldic painting on the tower came to light during the 1960s.

Turn right on Pfisterstraße to Platzl (Little Square), the site of a building of no great architectural distinction but the most publicised monument in Munich, the **Hofbräuhaus** (Royal Brewery) beer hall. Duke Wilhelm V founded a brewery in the Alter Hof in 1589 to avoid paying the high prices for imported beer from Hanover. Beer has always been just as much an aristocratic as a plebeian drink in Bavaria. It replaced wine as the staple alcoholic beverage after the Bavarian vineyards were destroyed by the cruel winters of the 13th and 14th centuries, making way for the sturdier hop and barley crops.

The brewery was first established in the royal bath house, and moved to these more spacious quarters in 1644. The Hofbräuhaus itself was built in 1896, after the brewery was transferred to the other side of the River Isar. It soon became the most prestigious of Munich's many political beer-hall arenas. In November 1921, Hitler's storm troops first gained notoriety in what became known as the *Schlacht im Hofbräuhaus* (Battle of the Hofbräuhaus). Today, the huge beer hall, with its long tables and oom-pah-pah music, is a magnet for tourists.

TO THE CITY GATES

Beyond Marienplatz and its immediate surroundings, there are many more sights to discover in Munich's Innenstadt (inner city). They're reached by following the main historic arteries leading from Marienplatz to the old city gates.

Eastwards to Isartor

Just south of the Hofbräuhaus, on the corner of Maderbräu-straße and Tal, another venerable Munich institution is the **Weißes Bräuhaus**, the beer hall/restaurant of the Schneider Brewery, known for its *Weißbier* (wheat beer) and Bavarian cuisine. Proceed eastwards along Tal to the **Isartor**, the only city gate that retains its original 14th-century dimensions. Put up in the days when the Bavarian Duke Ludwig IV was Holy Roman Emperor, a later fresco of 1835 on the gate shows him returning triumphantly from victory over the Habsburgs. Today, one of the towers houses a roof-top café and the **Valentin-Karlstadt-Musäum** (open Mon–Tues 11.01am–5.29pm, Fri–Sat 11.01am–5.59pm, Sun 10.01am–5.59pm), devoted to the famous cabaret comic star of 1920s Munich, Karl Valentin *(see below)* and his stage partner Liesl Karlstadt.

Valentin's Day

Although little known outside Germany, Karl Valentin was regarded by connoisseurs as a comic genius equal to Charlie Chaplin. While resident in Munich in the early 1920s, the dramatist Bertolt Brecht went almost every night to watch Valentin's portrayal of the clownish, working-class characters of peasant origin who were so peculiar to the city.

Munich's artists and intellectuals loved Valentin's insane, surreal logic. One of his most celebrated sketches portrayed an attempt to house birds in an aquarium and fish in a bird-cage.

Erasmus Grasser's *Moriskentänzer* in the Stadtmuseum

Münchner Stadtmuseum

The walk to Sendlinger Tor takes you past the municipal museum and through the busy shopping area of Sendlinger Straße. From the southeast corner of Marienplatz, follow Rindermarkt past St Peter's Church *(see page 35)*. The street soon widens into a square, the centre of which holds the **Rinderbrunnen** (cattle fountain), designed by Joseph Henselmann.

From here cut across Rosental and into St-Jakobs-Platz to visit the **Münchner Stadtmuseum** (Munich City Museum, open Tues–Sun 10am–6pm). It's well worth spending an hour or two here to get an overview of the town's development since the Middle Ages. In the Moriskenraum is displayed the museum's main attraction, the *Moriskentänzer*, wooden carvings of Morris Dancers taken from the Altes Rathaus council chamber. Dated 1480, they are magnificent examples of Erasmus Grasser's Gothic style. Maps, models and photographs on the first floor illustrate Munich's rich history. On the second floor are 20 rooms furnished colourfully in various decorative styles from the past. There are sumptuous rooms from the Residenz, as well as cosy bourgeois homes of the 19th century, furnished with *Biedermeier* or *Jugendstil* pieces. Highlights include a reconstruction of an 18th-century *Weinstube* (wine tavern) and an opulent artist's studio (Makart-Zimmer). The fashion collection illustrates the evolution of styles in a town that has long been a centre for design. Children (and adults, too) will love the **Puppentheater-Sammlung** (Puppet Theatre Collection), one of the largest of its kind in the world. Bavaria has long been a traditional centre for the production of glove-puppets and mechanical toys.

Just across the road the new **Jüdisches Museum München** (open Tues–Sun 10am–6pm) mirrors the many facets of Jewish culture in Munich over the past centuries.

Cross Oberanger and continue up the short Hermann-Sack-Straße to arrive in Sendlinger Straße. On the opposite side of the street, on the corner of Hackenstraße, is the impressive four-storey **Altes Hackerhaus**, the historic home of a traditional Munich restaurant, complete with inner courtyard. Go farther along Hackenstraße to the corner of Hotterstraße, where Munich's oldest operating tavern, **Gaststätte zur Hundskugel**, has been serving beer since 1440.

Asamkirche

Return to busy Sendlinger Straße. Amidst the shops on the right-hand side (No. 62) rises the famous Church of St John Nepomuk, better known as the **Asamkirche** after its creator, the Bavarian architect and sculptor Egid Quirin Asam (1692–1750). This master of late-baroque illusion had wanted to build his own private church here, but although he had taken over all the construction costs he was forced to make it accessible to the public after fierce resistance on the part of

Asamkirche interior

the citizens. The foundation stone was laid in 1733, and the consecration took place in 1746. Asam was assisted in the design by his brother, Cosmas Damian, who specialised in fresco painting. The result is one of the most astonishing achievements of Bavarian baroque. The interior is a theatrical masterpiece of sculpture, decoration and light; the **high altar** leads the eye up to a large Crucifixion dominated by a representation of God the Father wearing the papal crown.

Next door at No. 61 is the **Asamhaus**, where Egid Quirin lived. It was built at the same time as the church, and again with the assistance of Cosmas Damian. It's worth studying the intricate facade. Secure in their Catholic faith, the Asam brothers happily mixed pagan and Christian figures in their decorative schemes. Just below the roof to the right (directly above the doorway) you'll see a representation in stucco of heaven and the monogram of Christ. Below that appears the seated figure of Mary. To the left is a vine-bedecked Olympus, and Apollo is accompanied by the triumphant gods of Fame and Fortune. Pegasus leaps up to them while, lower down, a riot of nymphs and satyrs dance around the Muses of painting, sculpture and architecture.

At the end of Sendlinger Straße, only two hexagonal towers remain from the 14th-century **Sendlinger Tor**.

Fußgängerzone

West of Marienplatz, Kaufingerstraße leads into Neuhauser
Straße, both of them forming the longest section of Munich's
Fußgängerzone (pedestrian precinct), busy with shoppers and
popular with summertime buskers. At the corner of Neuhauser
Straße and Augustinerstraße is the former Augustinian church;
in Napoleonic times it became a customs house and much later,
in 1966, a museum of hunting and fishing, the **Deutsches
Jagd- und Fischereimuseum** (open daily 9.30am–5pm, Thur
until 9pm). Fronted by a wild boar in bronze, the collection
will fascinate hunters, anglers and children alike.

Further along Neuhauser Straße is the 16th-century **St
Michael's**, an Italian Renaissance church with baroque
overtones (the first of its kind in Germany), designed by the
Dutch architect Friedrich Sustris. St Michael's epitomises
the combative spirit of the Counter-Reformation, and it is
fitting that the Wittelsbach dukes and German emperors, the
secular defenders of the faith, are depicted on the gabled
facade. Above the entrance, third figure from the right,
stands the church's founder, Duke Wilhelm V (with a model
of the church in his hand).

The interior is a gigantic
Renaissance hall, 20m (66ft)
wide, with a barrel vaulted
ceiling; at the time of its
construction only St Peter's
in Rome was larger.

The nearby fountain, the
Richard Strauß-Brunnen,
with its sculpture group from
the opera *Salome*, commemorates Munich's best-known
musician, the composer of
world-famous operas.

**Wild boar outside the Hunting
and Fishing Museum**

The elegant Wittelsbacher Brunnen

Karlsplatz and Environs

Karlstor, a city gate dating from the 14th century, links Neuhauser Straße to the busy Karlsplatz, which is popularly known as Stachus after an innkeeper named Eustachius Föderl. **Stachus** conceals a veritable city of underground shops, which extends from the exit of the U- and S-Bahn station.

Walk north to Lenbachplatz and you'll find the city's loveliest fountain, the **Wittelsbacher Brunnen**, which was built in neo-baroque style by Adolf von Hildebrand at the end of the 19th century. Pacellistraße, to the east of Lenbachplatz, takes you past the baroque facade of the **Dreifaltigkeitskirche** (Trinity Church). In 1704 a young girl, Anna Maria Lindmayr, dreamt that Munich would be invaded and destroyed unless a new church were constructed. Sure enough, the next year, during the War of the Spanish Succession, Austrian soldiers arrived. Although work on the Dreifaltigkeitskirche did not begin until 1711, the town was saved from destruction.

Promenadeplatz is noted for the elegance of Palais Montgelas. This neoclassical building today forms part of the **Bayerischer Hof Hotel** *(see page 129)*.

Continue north along Kardinal-Faulhaber-Straße past the Palais Porcia, one of Munich's first baroque palaces, now a bank, to the **Erzbischöfliches Palais** (Archbishop's Palace) at No. 7, a triumph of rococo harmony. It's the only 18th-century palace built by François de Cuvilliés *(see page 48)* to have survived intact to the present day. A few steps to the north on Salvatorplatz, the **Literaturhaus** has become a new focus in Munich's cultural life, with it's lovely café-restaurant Dukatz *(see page 138)*.

THE RESIDENZ AND SURROUNDINGS

Max-Joseph-Platz is named after the king whose statue sits in the centre. The fourth Max-Joseph of the Wittelsbach dynasty and the first, thanks to Napoleon, to be king, wanted what he considered to be a more dignified standing pose. Unfortunately, he died before the statue was completed, so his son Ludwig I accepted the seated version.

The statue was put alongside the greatest monument of Max-Joseph's family, the Wittelsbach **Residenz**. In 1385 the citizenry revolted, driving the dukes to construct safer lodgings than the Alter Hof *(see page 37)*. More than five centuries later, in 1918, another group of rebellious citizens pounded on the Residenz doors during the revolution that resulted in the short-lived Bavarian Republic. The Wittelsbachs had to move out once again, and this time it was for good.

The Residenz, now a museum, shows just how wealthy the Bavarian principality grew to be. Successive members of the Wittelsbach dynasty expanded the original stronghold to create a complex of palaces around seven courtyards. The Königsbau or King's Tract, bordering the square on the north side, was only built in 1826–35, on the instructions of Ludwig I to house his appartments. Ludwig's architect, Leo von Klenze, adapted the designs of Karl von Fischer to create a heavily rusticated facade with 21 bays in the style of the Florentine Palazzo Pitti. Before entering the museum through the large central doors, note three other buildings on the square. Opposite stands the neoclassical former **Hauptpostamt**, or Main Post Office, also designed by Klenze and now with a restaurant under the arcades. Rebuilt in 1963, the **Nationaltheater**, Munich's opera house, closes off the east side of the square. It is a copy of the original building of 1818, a Greek-temple design by Karl von Fischer (first rebuilt by Leo von Klenze after a fire in 1825). Sandwiched between the Residenz and the opera house is the **Residenztheater**, which was built in 1948–51 by Karl Hocheder in place of the Cuvilliés-Theater *(see page 49)*.

Max-Joseph-Platz also marks the beginning of **Maximilian-straße**, Munich's most elegant avenue *(see page 67)*.

The Königsbau facade of the Residenz, designed by Leo von Klenze

Residenzmuseum and Treasury

The **Residenzmuseum** (open daily Apr 1–Oct 15: 9am–6pm; Oct 16–March 31: 10am–4pm, various morning and afternoon tours; fee; combination ticket for Residenzmuseum and Schatzkammer) can be visited independently or as part of a guided tour. There's a huge amount to see in the 112 rooms, halls and galleries, in addition to the 10 rooms of the Schatzkammer (Treasure Chamber). Here are the highlights:

Ahnengalerie (Gallery of the Ancestors). Here you can acquaint yourself with a mere 121 of the Wittelsbachs, starting with Duke Theodor, who lived around AD700.

Antiquarium. Designed by Friedrich Sustris for Duke Albrecht V in 1558, this is the largest and most beautiful Renaissance hall north of the Alps. The room takes its name from the 16th-century busts of ancient Greek and Roman leaders on display.

Porcelain collections. This prodigious array of French, English and German porcelain includes Meißen, from near Dresden, as well as local pieces produced in Nymphenburg *(see page 71)*. Japanese and Chinese porcelain and superb lacquer work form part of a separate exhibit.

Reiche Zimmer. Together these State Rooms provide the most outstanding example of rococo décor in Germany. Cuvilliés designed them in 1729, and his jewel among jewels was the Grüne Galerie (Green Gallery). The Spiegelkabinett (Cabinet of Mirrors), Miniaturenkabinett and Chinesisches Kabinett are equally fascinating.

Hofkapelle and Reiche Kapelle. Of these intimate chapels, the first was originally set aside for common courtiers, while the second was for the exclusive use of the Wittelsbachs.

Grottenhof. Designed by Sustris in 1581, this is perhaps the most elegant courtyard in the Residenz, distinguished by the graceful arcade along the eastern side and by Hubert Gerhard's fine bronze Perseus fountain set in the middle. The

Grottenwand, or Grotto Wall (with a fountain in an alcove), gives the courtyard its name. A statue of Mercury is flanked by Nubian slaves, fish-tailed satyrs, nymphs and parrots, and the ensemble is encrusted with thousands of mussel, scallop and winkle shells.

Schatzkammer (Treasury). A separate tour is dedicated to viewing the dynasty's spectacular collection of jewellery, gold, silver, crystal and enamelware, amassed over the course of 1,000 years. One of the earliest of the Wittelsbach heirlooms is a communion goblet dating from about 890, known as the Arnulfziborium (Arnolph's Ciborium).

The Courtyards and Cuvilliés-Theater

Apart from the Grottenhof *(see above)*, all the courtyards of the Residenz can be visited free of charge by entering the complex via the older **Maximilian Residenz**, whose early 17th-century facade runs along Residenzstraße. The most attractive court-yard is the **Brunnenhof**, or Fountain Court, to the right of the entrance, which was built in the shape of a long, stretched octagon in 1620. The Wittelsbach fountain at its centre features Duke Otto von Wittelsbach with four mermen symbolising Bavaria's most important rivers at his feet.

From the Brunnenhof you can enter the enchanting Altes Residenztheater or **Cuvilliés-Theater** (separate admission). This rococo gem was originally located where

The Cuvilliés–Theater owes its survival to planning and foresight. In 1943, its stucco ornamentation and sculptures were dismantled. Some 30,000 pieces were carried away and stored in the vaults of various castles around Munich. Only six weeks later the theatre was gutted by fire bombs. However, 15 years elapsed before all the pieces were brought out of hiding and reassembled.

The Cuvilliés-Theater

the present Residenztheater stands and found its present location after World War II, when the Brunnenhof layout was reconstructed. Its architect, François de Cuvilliés the Elder, was a dwarf from the Spanish Netherlands, and the theatre is tiny, seating just 450 people. But its sense of festive intimacy turns every performance into a cosy gala. The four-tiered auditorium basks in gilded décor with hosts of Greek nymphs, gods and goddesses, and, with marvellous incongruity, an American Indian girl with her bow and arrows. The acoustics are warm and golden – totally suited to the Mozart works that have been performed here for the past 200 years.

Odeonsplatz

Residenzstraße leads out into **Odeonsplatz**, which forms a link between the inner city and Maxvorstadt and the university to the north. If you're coming from Marienplatz, you can also stroll along **Theatinerstraße**, which is pleasantly pedes-

The Theatinerkirche rising above the Feldherrnhalle

trianised and has a number of cafés with outdoor tables. Also look out for the entrance to the **Fünf Höfe**, a high-class shopping arcade with some top names in designer fashion. Adjacent is the **Hypo-Kunsthalle** (open daily 10am–8pm), venue for high-quality and innovative temporary art exhibitions.

Odeonsplatz is dominated on the west by the twin towers and dome of the **Theatinerkirche**. This splendid Italian baroque church was built in 1663–8 by two Italian architects, Agostino Barelli and Enrico Zuccalli. The facade was completed later by Cuvilliés. Perhaps because the church was built to celebrate the birth of a baby boy to Princess Henriette Adelaide, a feeling of jubilation animates its rich decoration – with sprigs of ornamental vines, acanthus leaves and rosettes in the most spirited Italian baroque style, and wonderful grey-and-white stucco embellishments in the cupola. Notice, as well, the triumphant pulpit, the high altar and, to the left, the Cajetan altar. This last was dedicated to St Cajetan, founder of the Theatine Order commemorated in the church's title.

Just across the street, facing Odeonsplatz, is the **Feldherrnhalle** (Hall of the Generals), a 19th-century monument to a number of Bavarian military leaders, including the Belgian-born Count Johann Tilly (a hero in the Thirty Years'

War) and Prince Karl-Philipp von Wrede, who achieved victory over the French in 1814. Less gloriously, it was the rendezvous for Nazi storm troops in Hitler's unsuccessful putsch of 1923, and was subsequently a focus for marches commemorating the event. Reinforcing the Italian atmosphere of the area, though with less of a light touch, the building is modelled after the Loggia dei Lanzi in Florence.

At the east side of the square an archway leads through to the Italian Renaissance-style **Hofgarten** (Court Garden), restored and replanted with the chestnut trees, flower beds and fountains specified in the original 17th-century plan. In the centre stands a 12-sided temple dedicated to Diana, topped by a bronze statue of Bavaria. The arcades that line the garden house art galleries and cafés, and are decorated with frescoes of historic scenes that feature the Wittelsbachs.

Ludwigstraße

Odeonsplatz leads into **Ludwigstraße**, which stretches north towards Schwabing *(see page 62)*. This grand avenue of neoclassical buildings, leading into what at the time was nothing but open countryside, was the crown prince, later king Ludwig I's, most eccentric project. He commissioned the buildings as far as Theresienstraße to the prolific Leo von Klenze; beyond that Friedrich von Gärtner took over with his designs for the Bavarian State Library and the University *(see page 62)*. An **equestrian statue of Ludwig I** stands at the beginning of his street, outside Klenze's noble **Leuchtenberg Palais**.

Playing in the Hofgarten

THE MUSEUM QUARTER

Königsplatz

To the northwest of the inner city, beyond the Alter Botanischer Garten, **Königsplatz** represents a convergence of the noblest and basest aspirations arising from the past several hundred years of Munich's history. When Ludwig I was still crown prince, he visualised the square as a second Acropolis, a vast open space surrounded by Classical temples. There was no particular reason for the choice of this site (no junction of roads, for example). Ludwig simply overrode the customary demands of urban planning, and soon had men working on widening the stately Brienner Straße, the street that took the royal family from the Residenz to Nymphenburg Palace.

Leo von Klenze

In the early 19th century Munich was transformed from a simple residence city to a truly international centre of art and culture. This is largely down to the collaboration of two men, King Ludwig I, avid art collector and fan of antiquity, and Leo von Klenze, his star architect. Klenze, who was also a noted painter and writer, created a glittering array of neoclassical buildings that cities even twice the size of Munich would have been proud to possess. His projects included the Glyptothek (1815), the rebuild of the Nationaltheater (1823), the Alte Pinakothek (1826), the Königstract of the Residenz (1826) and the Hauptpostamt (1834). Klenze, along with Friedrich von Gärtner, the sculptor Ludwig Schwanthaler and the painter Peter Cornelius, also gave shape to the Maxvorstadt between Munich and Schwabing, with the elegant Ludwigstraße as the main axis *(see page 51)*. He was also active outside Munich, most notably with his work on the New Hermitage in St Petersburg (1839).

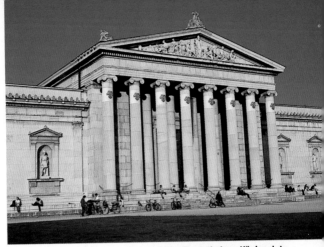

The Glyptothek on Königsplatz

With Leo von Klenze working as his architect, Ludwig turned the square into a grass-covered, tree-lined haven of tranquillity. A hundred years later, Hitler cut down the trees and paved over the grass for the troops and armoured cars of his military parades. (The pompous Nazi **Ehrentempel**, or Temple of Honour, which stood at the eastern end of the square, was deliberately blown up by the Allied military engineers in 1945.) Today, at last, Königsplatz has returned to its original serenity, and the pastoral greenery is back.

The U-Bahn station brings you out beside the **Propyläen** (Propylaeum), modelled after the entranceway to the Acropolis in Athens. Unlike the original, this splendid monument to Ludwig's sublime imperviousness to functional considerations does not lead anywhere, for it closes off Königsplatz rather than providing access to the square. Despite the Doric columns, it's not even authentically Greek, since the central gateway is flanked by two Egyptian-style pylons. The friezes

The Aeginates in the Glyptothek

that decorate them show the Wittelsbachs' special attachment to all things Greek: representations of the Greek war of liberation from the Turks, and of the Greek people paying homage to Ludwig's son Otto when he was made their king in 1832.

Situated on the south side of Königsplatz is the **Staatliche Antikensammlungen** (Classical Art Collections, open Tues–Sun 10am–5pm, Wed to 8pm, admission fee), a building which looks rather clumsy with its Corinthian columns set on an excessively elevated pedestal. The displays include a beautiful series of Greek vases and urns and, above all, the highly prized collection of Etruscan gold and silver formed by James Loeb. This German-American benefactor is known to students and scholars through the famous Loebs Classical Library of Greek and Latin texts.

Just across the square stands the companion building, the **Glyptothek** (open Tues–Sun 10am–5pm, Thur to 8pm, admission fee). It was designed in 1815 by von Klenze to display

Ludwig I's large collection of Greek and Roman sculpture, and was the first building to be planned for use as a public museum. Some 160 pieces, procured on the orders of the king, found a home in the massive, Ionic-columned edifice. The Glyptothek's greatest treasure is the sculpture from the gables of the Temple of Aphaia, found on the Greek island of Aegina. These well-preserved friezes, the *Aeginates*, have been dated to 505BC (west gable) and 485BC (east gable). On them are warriors with their shields, fighting to defend the island's patron goddess, smiling that rather smug Ancient Greek smile. Look for other works of major importance: the *Apollo of Tenea*, a *Medusa*, the goddess of peace *Irene* and the *Barberini Faun* (named after a 17th-century Italian family of classicists).

Lenbachhaus

Before crossing Königsplatz completely, go back through the Propyläen and cross the road to the **Lenbachhaus** on Luisenstraße. This elegant ochre-coloured villa, built in the 1880s in the style of the Florentine Renaissance, was originally the residence of Franz von Lenbach, a wealthy art collector. Today the villa houses the excellent **Städtische Galerie im Lenbachhaus** (Municipal Art Gallery, open Tues–Sun 10am–6pm, admission fee). This gives an overview of Munich painting from the Gothic period to the present day. The most important and popular collections, however, are those from the 19th and 20th centuries, and it now holds the largest collec-

When the U-Bahn at Königsplatz was built in the late 1970s, an enormous unused space between ground level and the station platforms was created. In 1994 this was converted for use as an art gallery; run as an annexe to the Municipal Gallery in the Lenbachhaus, the Kunstbau hosts prestigious temporary modern art exhibitions.

tion of Wassily Kandinsky paintings in Germany, in addition to canvases by Franz Marc, Gabriele Münter, Alexej von Jawlensky, August Macke and Paul Klee. These artists were the members of Munich's pre-World War I *Blaue Reiter* (Blue Rider) school of painting. The name derives from a blue-and-black horseman drawn by Kandinsky for an almanac in 1912. Horses and the colour blue were also dominant features of Franz Marc's work. The Lenbachhaus became a gallery for the *Blaue Reiter* collection in 1929.

Alongside these works the Lenbachhaus collections also include a number of works by Picasso, Braque, Dalí, the German Expressionists and a distinguished array of contemporary Americans.

The Lenbachhaus

The museum serves as a busy cultural centre, staging concerts, lectures and regular temporary exhibitions. On a hot summer day the lovely gardens and Mediterranean-style terrace are particularly inviting.

Führer's Buildings

Two surviving examples of Hitler's architectural contribution to the city, at the eastern end of Königsplatz, are known as the **Führerbauten** (Führer's Buildings). At Arcistraße 12, which now houses a music academy *(Musikhochschule)*, Hitler received Chamberlain and Daladier, the British and French prime ministers who accepted the infamous Munich Agreement of 1938 *(see page 27)*. Meiserstraße 10 today is home to some of Germany's most important archaeological and art-historical institutions, but it was built in 1933 as an administrative centre for the Nazi Party. These grim, bunker-like blocks, designed by Paul Ludwig Troost under the supervision of Hitler himself, ironically survived the American bombardments that severely damaged the historic Glyptothek and Staatliche Antikensammlungen.

Further down Meiserstraße is the **Alter Botanischer Garten**, whose lawns make for a pleasant stroll. Take a seat by the Neptune Fountain and look over the trees for a view of the two cupolas of the Frauenkirche. It's amazing to think that the people of Munich found time to lay out this lovely, tranquil spot right in the middle of the Napoleonic Wars.

Kunstareal München

Leave Königsplatz heading north along Arcisstraße and cross over Gabelsberger Straße to arrive at the Alte Pinakothek, the first of the triumvirate of major museums that make up what is referred to as the Kunstareal München (Munich Art Area).

Alte Pinakothek

Devoted to works from the 14th to the 18th centuries, the **Alte Pinakothek** (open Tues 10am–8pm, Wed–Sun 10am–5pm, admission fee; Sunday only €1) contains some of the world's finest collections of European paintings. It was built on the orders of Ludwig I to house the royal art collections, which had been acquired over the centuries by various dukes, electors and Bavarian Wittelsbach kings. The aquisitions of Ludwig himself form a signifcant portion of the museum's holdings. In all there are around 700 paintings on display.

Ludwig chose Leo von Klenze to provide a design for a monumental museum in the style of an Italian Renaissance

When it was opened in 1836, the Alte Pinakothek was the biggest painting gallery in the world. One of the first purpose-built public galleries, it was organised around the different schools of art, and the hanging scheme remains largely the same today.

palace. Ludwig himself laid the foundation stone on 7 April 1826, Raphael's birthday. The building was badly damaged in World War II (the brick infil on the facade clearly shows where the bombs fell). Reconstruction in 1958 to repair the ravages of war preserved the spacious layout of galleries and introduced some excellent lighting. The staircase which used to be in the east-wing of the building was now integrated in the entrance hall.

The Alte Pinakothek is renowned for its early Dutch as well as early German Old Masters. The latter includes Albrecht Dürer's famous *Self Portrait in a Fur Coat* (1500) heralding the arrival the humanistic spirit of Italy's Renaissance in the medieval north, and his *Four Apostles*, which seems to reflect the turbulent times when the Reformation swept through Northern Europe. Another outstanding German piece is the *Altarpiece of the Church Fathers* (Kirchenväter-altar), painted in about 1483 by Michael Pacher. Have a look, too, at Albrecht Altdorfer's *Alexanderschlacht* (1529) which portrays Alexander's victory over Darius of Persia. The thousands of soldiers make this a miniaturist masterpiece

The scope and quality of the Flemish collection is unique, including as it does one of the world's finest collection of paintings by Peter Paul Rubens. His works, including the

Great Last Judgement and the *Rape of the Daughters of Leucippus*, hang in the large central room on the first floor. The Alte Pinakothek is also richly endowed with works by Italian masters: Giotto, Botticelli, Lippi, Ghirlandaio, Perugino, Raphael, Titian, Tintoretto and Tiepolo are all represented, as is Leonardo da Vinci with a small *Madonna with Child* painted when he was only 21. The Dutch are here two with Rembrandt and Franz Hals, and there is Germany's best collection of Spanish paintings, with El Greco, Velázquez and Murillo all represented, the latter with his popular 17th-century paintings of lively young rascals.

Neue Pinakothek

Opposite the Alte Pinakothek is the strikingly modern **Neue Pinakothek** (Open Mon, Thur–Sun 10am–5pm, Wed 10am–8pm, admission fee). The 'New Gallery' was also founded by

The Neue Pinakothek

Beckman Hall, Pinakothek der Moderne

Ludwig I to house his collection of contemporary art; the building was destroyed in World War II, however, and this elegant sandstone and granite structure designed by Alexander von Branca was opened as its replacement in 1981. The gallery today contains outstanding works of European art and sculpture from the late 18th to the beginning of the 20th century, ranging from the German Romanticism of Caspar David Friedrich to the Austrian *Jugendstil* of Gustav Klimt. The wonderful collection of French impressionists includes works by Monet, Manet, Degas, Pissaro and Renoir; Cézanne, Gauguin and van Gogh stand for the pioneers of the modern age.

Pinakothek der Moderne

Opposite the Alte Pinakothek on Barer Straße is the **Pinakothek der Moderne** (Open Tues, Wed, Sat, Sun 10am–5pm, Thur, Fri 10am–8pm, admission fee). Opened in 2002, this is the largest museum of art and design in Europe, bringing four major collections – Art, Design, Architecture and Work on Paper – under one roof, in the light and airy building designed by Stephan Braunfels. The various collections fan out from the central foyer area, under the so-called Rotunda.

Art. This world-class collection, ranging from the main avant-garde movements of the early 20th century to contemporary art, comprises paintings, sculptures, installations and new media. Prominent among the displays, and including some of the 'degenerate art' so despised by the Nazis, are works by artists of *Die Brücke* and the *Blauer Reiter*, and by Max Beckman, who is represented with the largest European collection of his works. Picasso is also represented, as are the surrealists Max Ernst, René Magritte and Salvador Dalí.

Design. A fascinating insight into various design schools from the pioneers of modernism to the present day, focusing on themes such as motor vehicle design, bent wood furniture and computer culture.

Architecture. Focusing mainly on German architecture, the collection includes architectural drawings dating back to the 16th century, as well as photographs, models and computer animations. Look out for works by Balthasar Neumann, Leo von Klenze, Erich Mendelsohn and Le Corbusier.

The Rotunda in the Pinakothek der Moderne

Work on Paper. The huge collection of prints and drawings is one of the most important in Germany, containing 400,000 works dating from the 15th century to the present and including old German and Dutch prints, Italian Renaissance drawings and 19th-century German drawings.

The Siegestor

SCHWABING

Ludwigstraße *(see page 51)* stretches precisely 1km from Odeonsplatz in the south to **Siegestor** (Victory Gate) at its northern end. This triumphal arch was designed for Ludwig I as a monument to the Bavarian army. In 1944 the arch was badly damaged, and in 1958 only partially restored, leaving the scars of war and a new inscription on the south side: *'Dem Sieg geweiht, im Krieg zerstört, zum Frieden mahnend'* ('Dedicated to victory, destroyed in war, exhorting to peace').

Just south of the Siegestor is the **University** and the little square with fountains Geschwister-Scholl-Platz, so named in memory of the brother and sister who died in the struggle against Hitler *(see pages 27–8)*. Across the street is **St Ludwig's**, a neo-romanesque church noted for the gigantic fresco of the *Last Judgement* in the choir, by Peter Cornelius (1836). It is the world's second-largest fresco – measuring 18m (60ft) by 11m (37ft) – after Michelangelo's in the Sistine Chapel.

Leopoldstraße

Siegestor marks the southern boundary of Munich's famously bohemian district of Schwabing. Its main shopping street and promenade, **Leopoldstraße**, has been commercialised by ice-cream parlours, fast-food outlets and bars, but the more idyllic, older part of Schwabing can be discovered easily in the side roads that lead off to the English Garden – Werneckstraße, for example, or Nikolaiplatz. Ainmillerstraße, on the west side of Leopoldstraße, was home to a number of turn-of-the-century painters and writers who played a major part in establishing Schwabing's legendary reputation as the artists' quarter of Munich. Both Ainmillerstraße and Hohenzollern-straße (Schwabing's foremost shopping street with its bou-tiques and arcades) have some magnificent *Jugendstil* facades.

Once you come upon Münchener Freiheit, a road junction and U-Bahn stop, follow Feilitzschstraße to **Wedekindplatz**, a centre of theatre, cabaret, and café life. Continue on to Wer-neckstraße and catch a glimpse of the **Suresnes-Schlösschen**, which is now the Catholic Academy, through the iron gates. It was built in 1718 for Prince Elector Maximilian Emanuel as a reminder of the 10 years he spent at the French château of the same name during the War of the Spanish Succession. It was remodelled several times in the 19th century; some of the stuc-co work of the original baroque structure can still be seen.

Schwabing's Heyday

During Schwabing's heyday at the turn of the 20th century, artists and writers flocked to this bohemian area of Munich. Thomas Mann lived here, as did Frank Wedekind and Bertolt Brecht, Wassily Kandinsky and Paul Klee, as well as Franz Marc, Rainer Maria Rilke and symbol-ist poet Stefan George.

A countess-turned-Bohemian, Franziska zu Reventlow, chronicled the area's free love, free art and freedom for all in her novels. Schwabing was also home to the biting satirical weekly *Simplicissimus* and to the art magazine *Jugend*, which gave its name to *Jugendstil*, the German version of Art Nouveau.

In 1919, the 'Coffeehouse Anarchists', dramatist Ernst Toller and poet Erich Mühsam, took power after the assassination of the prime minister, Kurt Eisner. For all of six days – until the communists pushed the poets out – Schwabing ruled Bavaria, proclaiming the republic a 'meadow full of flowers'.

The Monopteros

Englischer Garten

From Schwabing, head east to the lovely **Englischer Garten**. Opened in 1793, the park was the brainchild of an American-born adventurer who had sided with the British in the American Revolution. Better known to the Bavarians as Count Rumford *(see page 19)*, Benjamin Thompson drew his inspiration from the famous English landscape gardeners Capability Brown and William Chambers. In fact, the **Chinesischer Turm** (Chinese Tower), a decorative pagoda that functions as a bandstand in the popular beer garden, owes a great deal to Chambers' Cantonese Pagoda in London's Kew Gardens. The natural landscaping is still a joy for visitors, including, famously, the nudists who stretch out either side of the Eisbach stream in the southern part of the park. The **Monopteros** (love temple) atop a grassy mound south of the Chinese Tower is an attractive focal point from which to admire the skyline of the inner city.

The gardens stretch almost 5km (3 miles) to the north. Stroll up to the **Kleinhesseloher See**, a boating pond with a café and beer garden on its eastern side; beyond, in the northern part of the park, you can walk beside the River Isar. In the southwest corner is the pretty **Japanese Tea House**, donated by Japan to commemorate the 1972 Olympic Games. Just beyond the Tea House, at Prinzregentenstraße 1, is the

Haus der Kunst (House of Art; open Mon–Sun 10am–8pm, Thur until 10pm; admission fee), a venue for temporary exhibitions and theatre. Originally called the Haus der Deutschen Kunst, this is another building of the Hitler era. Built as a temple to Hitler's personal vision of a truly German art, the monotonous construction, again by Paul Ludwig Troost, was soon nicknamed the 'Palazzo Kitschi' by Munich wits.

Prinzregentenstraße

Further along Prinzregentenstraße is the **Bayerisches Nationalmuseum** (open Tues–Sun 10am–5pm, Thur to 8pm, admission fee). Built in 1900, the exterior mirrors the artistic evolution of the periods exhibited inside – a Romanesque east wing, a later Renaissance western facade, a baroque tower and, finally, a rococo west wing. The collection spans German cultural history from the Middle Ages to the 19th century, emphasising both religious and secular arts and craftsmanship. One of the highlights is a collection of wooden sculptures by the Late Gothic master Tilman Riemenschneider.

Degenerates Forever

Hitler's speech inaugurating the Haus der Deutschen Kunst in 1937 attacked the 'obscenities' of avant-garde art and forbade any painter to use colours that the 'normal' eye could not perceive in nature. Two exhibitions were held to distinguish so-called great German art from that designated 'degenerate art'.

The trouble was that the 'degenerate' show was far more popular, and attracted 2 million visitors, five times as many as the other exhibition. Afterwards, many of these paintings, including works by Kandinsky, Mondrian, Kokoschka, and Chagall, were hidden away or sold abroad for valuable foreign currency. Today, some of these works are on display again in the Pinakothek der Moderne.

Just around the corner in Lerchenfeldstraße is the **Archäologische Staatssammlung** (Archaeological Museum), devoted to Bavarian finds from the earliest times. Now walk across Prinzregentenbrücke, crossing the river to the **Friedensengel** (Angel of Peace), high on her pillar. Begun in 1896, the monument celebrates the 25 years of peace that followed the German defeat of the French in 1871. Portraits of the architects of that peace – Bismarck, Kaisers Wilhelm I and II, and the generals Moltke and von der Tann – decorate the monument. The mosaics of *Peace, War, Victory* and the *Blessings of Culture* indicate the rather ambiguous nature of the celebration.

There's nothing ambiguous, however, about the **Villa Stuck**, at Prinzregentenstraße 60, which was built in 1898 for the last in Munich's line of painter-princes, Franz von Stuck. He amassed a fortune rivalling that of Franz von Lenbach *(see page 55)* by combining the new artistic trends of *Jugendstil* symbolism with the prevailing salon taste, which demanded a certain luxury spiced with just a dash of decadence. His opulent villa is the perfect setting for the **Jugendstil Museum**, which is housed here. All the interior decoration and furniture date from the turn of the 20th century. The house is guarded by Stuck's imposing equestrian *Amazone*, and is often used as a venue for temporary exhibitions.

The Maximilianeum

ALONG THE ISAR

South of the Friedensengel, the banks of the River Isar make for a pleasant stroll. Paths wind their way through parkland and along boardwalks just above the river. Above the Maximiliansbrücke looms the imposing neo-Romanesque facade of the **Maximilianeum**. Completed in 1874, the building was first the home of the Maximilianeum Foundation for Gifted Bavarian Students before becoming seat of the Bavarian Parliament in 1949. At the other side of the bridge, elegant **Maximilianstraße** leads towards the city centre. The street is named after its creator, Maximilian II (1848–64), who had it

At the edge of Haidhausen, above the River Isar, is the Kulturzentrum am Gasteig. Opened in 1985, this is one of the premier cultural venues in the city. It has a variety of concert halls and theatres, and is home to the acclaimed Munich Philharmonic Orchestra.

lined with buildings designed in a unique Gothic-Renaissance style known as the 'Maximilian style'. Notable structures include the **Völkerkundemuseum** (Ethnology Museum) and the **Upper Bavarian Goverment** building opposite; closer into town, at the other side of the inner ring road, is the renowned **Hotel Vier Jahreszeiten**; at this point, before Max-Josef-Platz *(see page 45)*, Maximilianstraße becomes the most elegant shopping street in the city.

East of the Maximilianeum is the district of **Haidhausen**. At one time this was a poor working-class area, but it now rivals Schwabing as Munich's trendiest quarter, with pleasant streets and plenty of good restaurants, cafés and nightspots.

Deutsches Museum

Below Gasteig *(see panel above)*, the path along the Isar passes the **Müllersches Volksbad**, the oldest public baths in Munich completed in 1901. With its opulent *Jugendstil* décor, it's a fine place for a swim and sauna *(see picture on page 89)*.

To the south, across the bridge and occupying its own island in the river, is the **Deutsches Museum** (open daily

9am–5pm, admission fee). With an exhibition area of over 5 hectares (12½ acres), this is the largest museum of science and technology in Europe. It was established by the engineer Oskar von Miller in 1903, and opened on its present, purpose-built site in 1925. From the outset, the intention was to entertain as well as educate, so the museum is not just a series of static displays, but hands-on with models, experimental machines and audio-visual effects that can nearly all be operated by visitors pushing buttons, turning wheels and pulling levers.

Oskar von Miller wanted a museum for all branches of technology and the natural sciences, aiming to show both historic developments and the very latest advances. Setting the tone, just outside the main entrance is 'the world's first vertical take-off jet transport plane', the Dornier Do 31 of 1967. This is no model, but the actual aircraft.

A Junkers Ju 52 in the Aeronautics Hall at the Deutsches Museum

It would take days if not weeks to see everything in the museum, which is divided into sections for the various classical fields of technology such as mining, road and bridge building, metallurgy and marine navigation, as well as forms of overland transport – from the carriage to the car. Here you can see the world's first automobile – the Benz Welding three-wheeler. Train enthusiasts will love the first German *Lokomobil*, built in 1862 and still operating. British visitors may note with interest that the Germans have on display a replica of *Puffing Billy*, one of the earliest English locomotives, dating from 1813. The Power Machinery section is also very popular, with its collection of impressive engines and turbines. The Marine Navigation department covers everything from the earliest dug-out canoes to developments in modern shipbuilding, the highlight being the 19th-century fishing boat *Maria*, exhibited alongside an Arab *dhow*.

The first floor is dominated by the department of Aeronautics: ordinary balloons, helicopters and jet aeroplanes are exhibited beside celebrities such as Lilienthal's original glider and the legendary Junkers Ju 52, plus an A4 rocket which forms a link with the department of Astronautics. On this floor also, the departments of Physics and Chemistry provide plenty of interactive materials, along with historical artefacts such as the telescope used to discover Neptune. Also worth a look are the Musical Instruments and Automata exhibition and, on the second floor, an exact replica of the prehistoric paintings of the Altamira Cave in Spain.

Much space is devoted to electricity, perhaps because Oskar von Miller himself made important contributions to electrical engineering. One of the main attractions of the museum is the thrice-daily demonstration of a high-voltage apparatus which simulates a stroke of lightning.

Schloss Nymphenburg

OUTSIDE THE CITY CENTRE

Schloss Nymphenburg

Away from the heat of the Residenz in the city centre, **Schloss Nymphenburg** (open daily Apr 1–Oct 15: 9am–6pm; Oct 16–March 31: 10am–4pm; admission fee) was the Wittelsbachs' summer refuge. This gleaming palace is set in extensive grounds with fountains, ponds and four garden pavilions – it's the perfect place for a stroll. There's no U-Bahn station at the palace, but a No. 17 tram or No. 51 bus will take you there.

Together with the Theatinerkirche *(see page 50)*, it was built to celebrate the birth of a new son and heir, Maximilian Emanuel, to Princess Henriette Adelaide in 1662. The palace had modest beginnings as a small summer villa, but it grew over the next century as each succeeding ruler added another wing or his own pavilion and changed the landscaping.

The palace is approached by a long canal with avenues on either bank leading to a semicircle of lawns, the Schlossron-

Lola Montez in the Schönheitsgalerie

dell, which is the site of the building containing the Royal Porcelain Factory *(see Shopping, page 87)*. In the central edifice of the palace proper are galleries of fine 18th-century stucco work and ceiling frescoes. The majestic two-storey banquet hall, **Steinerner Saal** (Stone Hall), contains some lively frescoes by Johann Baptist Zimmermann on the theme *Nymphen huldigen der Göttin Flora* (Nymphs Pay Homage to the Goddess Flora).

To the south, the first pavilion is the home of the famous **Schönheitsgalerie** (Gallery of Beautiful Women). Ludwig I commissioned Joseph Stieler to paint these portraits of Munich's most beautiful young women, including Ludwig's mistress, the dancer Lola Montez; daughter of an Irish adventurer and a Spanish countess, she went on stage as Señora María de los Dolores Porris y Móntez *(see page 21)*.

The **Marstallmuseum**, a dazzling collection of state coaches has been installed in the south wing, in what was once the royal stables. Starting from the extravagance of Karl Albrecht's 18th-century coronation coaches, the vehicles went on to achieve a state of ornamental delirium under Ludwig II. Look for his Nymphenschlitten (Nymph sleigh), designed for escapades in the Alps. On the first floor is the beautiful **Bäuml** collection of Nymphenburg porcelain, covering examples of the entire output from the Nymphenburg factory, from the early days in the 18th century to the 1920s.

Also in the Nymphenburg palace is the extensive **Museum Mensch und Natur** (Man and Nature Museum, open Tues–Sun 9am–5pm, admission fee), which covers the history of the planet and life on earth. The position of man in the universe and his responsibilities towards the environment are important themes, and numerous ecological topics are explored, such as land erosion, population growth and hunger.

The **gardens** were originally laid out in a subdued Italian style for Henriette Adelaide, but later lost some of their formality. They are decorated here and there with marble statues of Greek gods by Dominikus Auliczek and others.

Off to the left lies the **Amalienburg**, one of the prettiest little hunting lodges in Germany, built in 1734–9 by François de Cuvilliés, with the help of sculptor Joachim Dietrich and stucco artist Johann Baptist Zimmermann. Wander round the rooms where the hunting dogs and rifles were kept, the Pheasant Room next to the blue and white Dutch-tiled kitchen and, above all, enjoy the brilliant silver and pastel-yellow rococo **Spiegelsaal** (Hall of Mirrors). This was originally the pavilion's entrance.

Continue west to find the **Badenburg** (Bath Pavilion), fitted with fine Delft china fixtures. The **Großer See** is a large pond dotted with islands; overlooking it is a

Steinener Saal ceiling

love temple modelled after Rome's Temple of Vesta, goddess of fire. North of the central canal, with its spectacular cascade of water, is another, smaller pond. On the far side of it stands the **Pagodenburg**, an octagonal tea pavilion. The fourth of the park's pavilions is the **Magdalenenklause** (Hermitage), built for Maximilian Emanuel in 1725. Don't be surprised that the building is a crumbling ruin; the cracks and flaking plaster were deliberately incorporated into the mock Romanesque and Gothic structure, and a Moorish minaret was thrown in too.

Botanical Gardens and Schloss Blutenburg

The area lying north of the park is occupied by the **Botanischer Garten** (Botanical Gardens; tram No. 17, open daily), entered from Menzinger Straße. The Arboretum at the west end has been landscaped to resemble different climatic regions of the world, complete with their appropriate flora.

Farther west (No. 73 bus from Botan. Garten) is the medieval **Schloss Blutenburg**, worth visiting for its superb Late Gothic chapel. The three altars display splendid paintings by Jan Polack (1491): the *Holy Trinity* (high altar), *Christ Enthroned* (on the left) and the *Annunciation* (to the right). On the walls are hung some beautiful polychrome wooden sculptures (c. 1500) of the Apostles, Mary and a resurrected Christ. Within the castle, tasty food is served at the Schlossschänke Blutenburg, a cosy restaurant with beer garden. The castle also houses the International Youth Library.

> Fröttmaning, in the north of the city, is home of the 66,000-seat Allianz Arena, built for the 2006 World Cup and as the new home ground for the city's two football teams, *FC Bayern München* and *TSV 1860 München*. Its futuristic design enables it to change colour according to which team is playing. To get there take the U6 from Marienplatz.

Olympiapark

In the north of the city, best accessed via the U-Bahn (U3 from Marienplatz), is the sport and recreation area of the **Olympia-park** (Olympic Park), created for the 1972 Olympic Games. The complex is dominated by the 290m (950ft) high **Olympiaturm**, which was a symbol of those games. The restaurant and observation decks provide spectacular views of the city and surroundings, and on a clear day the Alps can seem almost close enough to touch. The other major feature of the complex is the **Olympiastadion**, with its 78,000 seating capacity and extraordinary tent-roof structure, designed by Behnisch and Partners. This used to be the home of Bayern Munich *(see opposite)*. The latest attraction here is **Sea Life Munich** (open daily from 10am), which provides a close-up look at underwater life along the Isar and Danube rivers, into the Black Sea and the Mediterranean.

Olympiapark

At the other side of the ring road is the distinctive main headquarters building of the car maker BMW. The bowl-shaped building in front is the **BMW Museum** (closed for revamp until spring 2008), which provides a fascinating insight into the history of the Bavarian Motor Works, with exhibits of cars, motorcycles and aircraft engines. The futuristic **BMW Welt** showroom complex is another attraction.

The parish church at Ramsau, near Berchtesgaden

EXCURSIONS

The Bavarian countryside is at its most beautiful to the south of the city. This is the land of dramatic mountains, picturesque lakes, onion-domed churches and Ludwig II's crazy castles. Visitors without a car can take a tour organised by the Munich-Upper Bavaria Tourist Office *(see page 126).*

Neuschwanstein

To reach Bavaria's most famous attraction, Neuschwanstein Castle, first follow the A96 and B12 to **Landsberg am Lech** (with its interesting medieval town centre), and then take the B17, the Deutsche Alpenstraße (German Alpine Road). Stop off at Steingaden to visit the lovely **St Johann Baptist Church**, which retains much of its 12th-century Romanesque exterior. You'll also enjoy the pleasant walk in the old cloister.

From Steingaden, it's worth making a detour just to the east of the B17 to visit the magnificent **Wieskirche** (Church in the Meadow), a pilgrimage church of 1754 designed by Dominikus Zimmermann. The church's ceiling is decorated with a sublime fresco by his brother Johann Baptist, which depicts Christ dispensing divine mercy. In its architecture and decoration, the church is a consummate work – perfect to the last rococo detail.

Return to the main road for the journey to the more pagan **Neuschwanstein** (follow the signs to the castle or look for signs to Füssen). A visit in 1867 to the medieval castle of Wartburg, Thuringia, first fired Ludwig's imagination with a vision of the Minnesänger, the minstrels of the 12th century, and he decided to build a castle that would recapture the aura of that romantic era. Ludwig replaced a ruined mountain retreat of his father's in the Schwangau with an extraordinary white-turreted castle. Set in the midst of a forest of firs and pines, it overlooks the gorge of Pöllat and Lake Forggen. Be sure to visit the throne room, and try to imagine, as did Ludwig, the minstrel contests of another age in the Sängersaal. Wagnerians will recognise the sculptural and painted allusions to *Tannhäuser*, *Die Meistersinger von Nürnberg* and *Tristan und Isolde*.

Tickets for both Neuschwanstein *(below)* and Hohenschwangau must be purchased at the Ticket-Center in Hohenschwangau, showing the exact admission times. Online tickets are also available (<www.hohenschwangau.de>)

While Neuschwanstein castle was being built, Ludwig kept an eye on its progress from the neighbouring

Oberammergau

castle of **Hohenschwangau**, just 1km (½ mile) away. This Neo-Gothic building had been constructed by his father, Maximilian II. In fact, Neuschwanstein and Hohenschwangau collectively are known as 'die Königsschlösser'. Take a look at the music room, with its display of Wagner memorabilia (the composer stayed at Hohenschwangau) and Ludwig's bedroom, noted for its star-studded ceiling.

Oberammergau and Linderhof

To reach the second of Ludwig's dream castles, take the Garmisch-Partenkirchen Autobahn from Munich, turning off west to **Ettal**. This lovely Benedictine monastery is set in a gently curving valley. Stop and admire Johann Jakob Zeiller's 18th-century fresco of the life of St Benedict. Then go on to **Oberammergau**, setting for the famous 10-yearly Passion Play, inaugurated in the plague year of 1633. In the town are preserved some very attractive 18th-century facades, adorned with paintings by the so-called *Lüftlmaler* (air painter), Franz Zwinck.

Ludwig's favourite castle, **Linderhof**, was the embodiment of his baroque fantasies. The palace, inspired by Versailles, is opulent inside and out. Quite apart from the carefully tailored landscape of pond and park, you could be excused for thinking that the whole romantic Alpine backdrop had been created from Ludwig's imagination. Only the Venus Grotto, carved out of the mountainside and forming another Wagnerian motif from *Tannhäuser*, is in fact man-made.

The Lakes

Ammersee (35km/56 miles southwest of Munich on the A96) is a delightful place for long walks along the lake or up into the wooded hills. Make for the Benedictine Abbey of **Andechs** that overlooks Ammersee from the east. The 15th-century church was was redecorated in the rococo style by Johann Baptist Zimmermann. The monastery brewery produces first-rate beer and is very popular for its beer garden.

For **Starnberger See**, the best route is by S-Bahn or by car along the Garmisch-Partenkirchen Autobahn. Relax in the area's quiet, rural scenery and wander along the peaceful rush-fringed shoreline. It was here that Ludwig II drowned in 1886 *(see pages 22–3)* after being held at Schloss Berg on the east shore, south of the wealthy provincial town of Starnberg.

The Bavarian Alps

On a clear day, particularly during *Föhn (see page 107)*, the Alps provide a stunning backdrop to the Bavarian countryside and are a playground for hikers and climbers, skiers, paragliders and even sailors and windsurfers. Though lower than some of the mountains in neighbouring Austria, they are nonetheless impressive, with steep limestone ridges running from west to east. In the west they begin with the lower **Allgäu Alps**, where Neuschwanstein is located, but these soon give way to the highest section, the Wetterstein range, which culminates in Germany's highest mountain, the **Zugspitze**. Its 2,962m/9,718ft summit can be reached by cable car or the Zugspitzbahn railway from **Garmisch**. A break in the mountains is occupied by the picturesque town of **Mittenwald**, above which rise the impressive **Karwendel Mountains** (mostly in Austria). Further to the east, just beyond Chiemsee, the most spectacular scenery of all can be found around **Berchtesgaden** with the east face of the mighty Watzmann (2,713m/8,901ft) towering over the deep turquoise **Königsee**.

► **Chiemsee** (to the southeast of Munich on the Salzburg Autobahn) is the largest lake in Bavaria and the location of Ludwig II's most ambitious castle. **Herrenchiemsee** is situated on an island, the Herreninsel, at the western end of the lake and reached by ferry. Ludwig started work on it in 1878, but ran out of money and time, in 1886. Nevertheless, he made a valiant attempt at recreating the grandeur of Versailles, and the magnificent **Spiegelsaal** (Hall of Mirrors) can certainly bear comparison with the Galerie des Glaces. It is a homage to the king Ludwig admired most, Louis XIV. On a tiny island nearby is **Frauenchiemsee** where Duke Tassilo III founded a Benedictine convent in 782. As well as the former convent there are some charming little fishing cottages and rstaurants.

Chiemsee

Turn right off the Salzburg Autobahn just before the Austrian border to reach **Berchtesgaden**. The town's ancient prosperity depended on salt, and visitors can enjoy a thrilling trip into the depths of the old **Salzbergwerk** (salt mines). The splendour of the surroundings was appreciated not least by Hitler, who had his Eagle's Nest perched atop the nearby **Kehlstein**. The landscape is dominated by the mighty **Watzmann**, whose east face plunges almost 2000m (6,500ft) into the deep turquoise waters of **Königsee**, Bavaria's most beautiful lake.   ◄

North of Munich

Dachau (17km/11 miles northwest of Munich on the B304, or take the S-Bahn, Line 2) used to be known primarily for the remains of a 16th-century château and its fine 18th-century facades. Then, on 20 March 1933, after Hitler had been in power for a mere 48 days, Dachau was designated as the site of the first Nazi concentration camp. Today, while you can still appreciate the charming town centre, you

Watchtowers at Dachau

should also visit the **Concentration Camp Museum** (open Tues–Sun 9am–5pm, free) built on the site of the camp. You can take a bus or taxi from the S-Bahn station. Exhibitions document the camp's sinister history. Dachau was not an extermination camp but served as a detention centre for political prisoners; even so, 31,951 deaths were recorded between 1933 and 1945. In addition to the museum, you can see the original crematorium and gas chambers (labelled 'Bad' for showers), built but never used, as well as reconstructed prison barracks.

Continue east to **Schloss Schleißheim** and re-enter the baroque world of Maximilian Emanuel. The Neues Schloss has a glorious staircase with frescoes by Cosmas Damian Asam. Beautiful stucco work adorns banqueting halls and galleries such as the Barockgalerie, containing a fine collection of 17th-century Dutch and Flemish paintings. The **gardens**, complete with waterfall and canals, are a triumph of French landscape design. Make a point of visiting the **Schloss Lustheim** hunting lodge at the eastern end.

WHAT TO DO

CONCERTS AND OPERA

Munich has no problem in providing entertainment – there's something here to suit every taste. First and foremost, Munich is a city of music, with four major symphony orchestras: the Bavarian State Orchestra, Munich Philharmonic, Bavarian Radio Symphony and Graunke Symphony Orchestra. The main concerts are performed at the **Kulturzentrum am Gasteig** *(see page 68)*, an enormous complex that incorporates several concert halls under one roof.

In summer there are open-air concerts on Odeonsplatz and Königsplatz, or you can enjoy performances in the palatial setting of Nymphenburg, Blutenburg, or Schleißheim. Music does not stop during the winter, when concerts are performed in the Frauenkirche and many other churches in town.

A Munich Season (Münchner Saison) from December to February offers the special joy of Mozart operas in the Cuvilliés-Theater. In summer, open-air opera is staged in the pleasant Brunnenhof courtyard of the gigantic Residenz.

Opera has been an attraction in Munich for centuries. The town vies with Bayreuth for performances of Wagner, and the works of Mozart and Richard Strauß are favourites. Though the Italians take second place, Verdi, Rossini and Donizetti are by no means neglected. The majestic Nationaltheater makes every opera evening seem like a gala. The Bavarian State Orchestra plays under the world's greatest conductors, and the summer festival *(Münchner Opernfestspiele)* in July and August attracts the very best international singers.

A performance in the Philharmonie at Gasteig

Jazz is a favourite in Munich; internationally acclaimed musicians play nightly in many places, most notably at the Unterfahrt im Einstein, Einsteinstraße 42, and at Mister B's, Herzog-Heinrich-Straße 38, both in Haidhausen. In summer you can also find jazz and dixie musicians playing at the Waldwirtschaft beer garden.

Munich is a major venue for **rock and pop concerts**, attracting a steady stream of international artists. The biggest bands play in the Olympic Stadium; other venues include the Olympiahalle, the Muffathalle, Schlachthof, Elserhalle and Backstage. The **Tollwood Festival**, Munich's lively outdoor festival of music, theatre and art, held in the southern part of the Olympia Park in June and July, attracts well-known international bands and World Music artists to its concert tent.

To find out what's happening when you're in Munich, get hold of a copy of the monthly programme from the Tourist Office or visit <www.munich-tourist.de>; another useful source of information is the monthly English-language magazine, *Munich Found* (<www.munichfound.de>).

Nightlife

The area around Münchener Freiheit in Schwabing is the best known nightlife district; Feilitzstraße and Occamstraße are lined with clubs, discos, and pubs. Haidhausen is Munich's other 'in' area. The Glockenbachviertel, located south of Sendlinger Tor, is the focus of the gay scene, and nearby, on the streets radiating from Gärtnerplatz, a large number of hip new bars have opened up. Top nightclubs include the Alabamahalle at Domagkstraße 33, with varied club nights in a massive space. Optimolwerke at Friedenstraße 10 and Die Kultfabrik at Grafinger Straße 6 (both near Ostbahnhof) are Munich's biggest party zones with buzzing clubs, bars and live concerts. Far more intimate, the Atomic Café at Neuturmstraße 5 is a trendy spot in the city centre.

In one of the beer tents at the Oktoberfest

FESTIVALS

The people of Munich always seem to have something to celebrate. More than 100 days a year are officially given over to festivals, processions, banquets and street dances commemorating events such as the arrival of the first strong beer of the year *(Starkbierzeit)* or the departure – several centuries ago! – of this plague or that occupying army. In fact, any excuse will do.

Fasching (carnival) is almost as mad in Munich as it is in the Rhineland. It runs from 7 January. Some 2,500 balls are held all over town for policemen and doctors, lawyers and butchers, artists and plumbers. There are masked processions, and market women at the Viktualienmarkt have their fling at midday on Shrove Tuesday.

The biggest blow-out of all is the **Oktoberfest**. This began when the Crown Prince Ludwig (later Ludwig I) celebrated his marriage to Princess Theresa in October 1810 with a

Prost! from the Oktoberfest

horse race, to which everybody came. They came again the next year, too, and the year after, and they're still coming from all over the world. Although the horse race has been dropped and the festivities now take place during the warmer second half of September, the blushing bride is not forgotten – the name of the site on which the Oktoberfest is held is Theresienwiese, west of the city centre. Locals, however, refer to it as the *Wies'n*, which is also a nickname for the festival. The festival begins with a procession of *Wies'n* brewers and innkeepers with their splendidly decorated beer wagons followed by the one carrying the Festival Queen. For two weeks after the mayor has tapped the first barrel, revellers consume gargantuan quantities of beer, toted around 10 litres at a time by the energetic beermaids. This brew washes down hundreds of thousands of barbecued chickens and thousands of sausages, and the operator of a monster roasting spit boasts that he turns out up to 60 whole oxen during the festival. And to work all that off, there's the fun of the fair, with roller-coasters, giant ferris-wheel and dodgem cars.

SHOPPING

Munich is an elegant town, the capital of Germany's fashion industry, so there's no lack of chic boutiques, especially on **Theatinerstraße**, **Maximilianstraße**, and on Schwabing's **Leopoldstraße**. The **Fünf Höfe** (Five Courtyards) shopping precinct between Theatinerstraße and Kardinal-Faulhaber-Straße is another ultra-chic address.

Munich is also the place for the world's best selection of well-tailored garments (coats, jackets and suits) made in Loden cloth, a Bavarian speciality. This waterproof wool fabric, originally developed for hunters, has kept the people of Munich warm for over a hundred years.

You may even care to try the Bavarian costume *(Tracht)*. There are smart green-collared grey jackets for men or, for women, gaily coloured *Dirndl* dresses with a full gathered skirt and fitted bodice. *Lederhosen*, those slap-happy traditional shorts for Bavarians, may amuse the children.

Nymphenburg porcelain is still turned out in traditional rococo designs. You can view pieces (and make a purchase) at the factory at Schloss Nymphenburg *(see page 72)* or in the Fünf Höfe. Connoisseurs should be on the look-out for old Meißen or modern Rosenthal.

German-made cutlery, kitchen utensils and electronic gadgets are of a very high standard and superbly designed. You might also like to consider linens, in modern or traditional designs, which are renowned for their good old-fashioned quality. A great way to save on winter heating bills is to invest in a sumptuous duck- or goose-down *Federbett* or eiderdown, another good buy.

Fashion born in Munich: the Escada shop on Theatinerstraße

The 'Auer Dult' is a seasonal fleamarket dating back to the 14th century. It takes place over nine days, three times a year (May, July and October) in the Au district (around Mariahilfplatz, south of the Deutsches Museum). There are invariably some interesting bargains to be had.

Germany remains at the forefront of quality optical equipment manufacture, and its famous-name brands are still very visible in binoculars, cameras and camcorders.

The country has always produced excellent children's toys; its industrial prowess is reflected in the intricate building sets and model trains.

The presence of so many great orchestras and musicians in Germany means that the selection of records here is probably second only to the United States. The production of musical instruments, such as the finest grand pianos, violins, and even harmonicas, also enjoys a venerable reputation.

SPORTS

The city's great boon to sports lovers was the construction of the Olympic facilities in 1972. All year round, ice-skating fans congregate at the Olympic ice rink. The swimming pool at the Olympia Schwimmhalle can be used by anyone, as can about a dozen other indoor as well as open-air pools (Freibäder) dotted around the city. The outdoor pools, which open in May, are a summertime institution in Munich; they are superbly maintained and all provide lawns for sunbathing. Most of the indoor pools are equipped with saunas and other wellness facilities; the Cosimabad in Bogenhausen has a wave pool and the award-winning Westbad has a 60-m slide. The Dante-Winter-Warmfreibad has a heated outdoor pool, which attracts many people even in snowy winters.

Munich has its share of tennis courts, too: the best are at Olympiapark and in the Englischer Garten.

While serious runners might want to hit the track in the Olympic Stadium, jogging and running in the Englischer Garten is more fun, especially the stretch along the River Isar. Running in the city is also pleasant, as long as you get out early enough (before 7am) to avoid the traffic. For some good exercise and lovely scenery, try cycling the 14km (9 miles) along the river path to Ismaning, or any of the bike routes throughout Munich. For people who don't want to exert themselves, delightful raft trips *(Floßfahrten)* are organised at weekends. You can drift slowly down the Isar from Wolfratshausen to Munich, while the beer flows and brass bands play. It is recommended to book as early as possible (<www.schrall.com>).

There are 15 golf courses located within a radius of 20km (12 miles) around the city. Courses in the Munich area include Eichenried, Feldafing, Olching, Wörthsee and Margarethenhof am Tegernsee.

The Volksbad in Haidhausen, a wonderful *Jugendstil* experience

Farther out of Munich you can do some serious sailing or windsurfing on Ammersee, Starnberger See, Tegernsee and Chiemsee. The local lakes and rivers also offer good fishing.

Hiking is a major pastime, especially as you approach the Bavarian Alps. Just 97km (61 miles) from Munich, Garmisch-Partenkirchen provides guides for mountain climbing. There are plenty of peaks to tackle, including the 2,962-m (9,717-ft) high Zugspitze. Once you are in the Alps, the whole range of winter sports is at your disposal. Garmisch has, in addition to skiing (and a very professional ski school), its own Olympic rink for skating and ice hockey. The more sedate can try curling, and for the more adventurous there is a bob-sled run.

MUNICH FOR CHILDREN

Munich, complete with fairytale buildings, parks and gardens, is a wonderful city for children, at any time of year and in any weather. Many of the museums are suitable for children, but the **Deutsches Museum** *(see page 68)* is the biggest hit by far, with plenty of fascinating machines and models to play with, and hands-on exhibits for children to operate for themselves. Adults can accompany children aged 10 or under to the **Kinderreich** ('Kids' Kingdom')

A Day at the Zoo

If you feel like a change from cultural activity, try the delightful **Hellabrunn Zoo** (U3 U-Bahn or bus No 52 to Thalkirchen from Marienplatz). Here, animals are grouped according to their continent of origin, and you'll see zoological curiosities such as the tarpan, a kind of horse, and the white-tailed gnu. The antics of the chimps 'working out' in their own private gym attract appreciative audiences. It's possible to spend hours in the kids area alone, with pony rides and goat pens, plus a superb adventure playground and suspension bridge.

section, where they can explore a variety of scientific phenomena such as light, sound and energy, with apparatus ranging from a giant guitar to a waterfall.

The **Museum Mensch und Natur** *(see page 73)* is an excellent museum that explores a variety of issues on the subject of man, nature and ecology, and is full of weird and wonderful exhibits sure to keep youngsters of all ages entertained.

Soaking up the sun at the zoo

You could also try the **Marionette Collection** in the Stadtmuseum *(see page 40)*; the **Deutsches Jagd- und Fischereimuseum** (the Hunting and Fishing Museum, *see page 43*), with exhibits on game, hunting techniques, weapons and trophies, and the story of fishing equipment through the ages; and the **Spielzeugmuseum** (Toy Museum, *see page 33*) showing examples from 200 years of toys. **Sea Life** in the Olympiapark introduces children to the underwater environment of rivers and seas, while the BMW **Museum** re-opens in 2008 with some great new features. The **Siemens Forum** on Oskar-Von-Miller-Ring presents 140 years of electronics history in a fun, hands-on way.

Last but by no means least, south of the Zoo, at Geiselgasteig, is the **Bavaria Filmatelier** (Bavaria Film Studios), which appeals to children and adults alike. Some acclaimed international productions have been made here, including *Never Ending Story* (1984). The submarine used in *Das Boot*, the epic story of a submarine crew in World War II, is the centrepiece of the studio tour (daily 9am–4pm/last tour).

Calendar of Events

For the most up-to-date information on the city's festivals and arts calendar, including a current list of times and dates, ask the tourist information office for their monthly programme of events, or consult the local press.

7 January to Ash Wednesday *Fasching*. Costumed balls and processions.
Mid-March *Starkbierzeit*. Making and sampling of special strong beers during the week including 19 March (St Joseph's Day), always ending in '-ator' like Salvator.
End of April *Frühlingsfest* (Spring Fair). Fun fair, concerts. *Auer Dult*. Flea market, over nine days from the last Saturday in April (also in July and Oct).
Mid-June *Stadtgründungsfest* (Foundation of the City). Weekend around the 14th of June. Fun fair.
June *Corpus Christi*. Colourful street procession from the Frauenkirche to Maxvorstadt; people and horses wear traditional costumes.
End of June *Filmfest München* (Munich Film Festival, last week of June) at selected cinemas and Gasteig Culture Centre.
June/July *Tollwood Sommerfestival*. A three-week open-air extravaganza of music, art and theatre from around the world, held in the southern part of the Olympiapark.
June/July *Nymphenburger Schlosskonzerte*. Open-air concerts in the grounds of Schloss Nymphenburg.
3 weeks in July *Opernfestspiele*. A variety of opera performances that take place at the Nationaltheater and Cuvilliés-Theater.
September/October *Oktoberfest*. 16 days up to the first Sunday in October. Commemorates the marriage of Ludwig I to Princess Theresa in 1810. Beer drinking, hog roasts, fun fair and processions.
November *Six-Day-Cycle Race*. Two-wheeled marathon at the Olympiahalle. Entertainment, beer and food.
December *Christkindlmarkt* (Christmas market). Market offering crafts and gifts for the season on and around Marienplatz. Further markets at Münchner Freiheit, Weissenburger Platz and Rotkreuzplatz, and at the Chinese Tower in the English Garden. *Tollwood Winterfestival* at Theresienwiese.

EATING OUT

Eating and drinking in Bavaria in general, and in Munich in particular, are favourite leisure pursuits. Conviviality reigns supreme, both in the high temples of gastronomy and at the long, communal tables of the *Bräuhaus*, *Gaststätte*, *Gasthaus*, *Wirtschaft* and *Biergarten*.

WHERE TO EAT

With its great prosperity and tradition of good living, Munich has a great deal to offer gastronomically – indeed some of its sophisticated eateries, manned by award-winning chefs, are among the finest anywhere. In addition, the city remains a bastion of traditional Bavarian fare; you can tuck into your roast duck, chicken or pork with dumplings at the city's beer gardens, and there are still some very good Bavarian restaurants as well. Time was when international cuisine in Munich was almost exclusively Italian, Greek, Turkish and Balkan, but now you can get just about anything, a recent development being the surge in popularity of Indian and Afghan food, with some really excellent restaurants.

A famous Bavarian *Bräuhaus*

Munich's growing sophistication is such nowadays that elegance, however casual, is considered to be more important than the traditional formality of ties for men or skirts for women. It's a good idea to reserve a table in advance at the smarter places. Although a service charge of 15 percent is already included in the bill, not many people have been known to refuse a little extra.

Beer Halls and Beer Gardens

The niceties of dress and advance reservations are not a problem at the more popular *Gaststätte* or *Bräuhaus* – literally meaning 'brewery', but in actual fact a beer hall. These establishments usually serve full meals in addition to beer. All the great breweries have their own beer halls in Munich, and beer gardens, too. Some of the most popular beer gardens are in the Englischer Garten, at the Chinese Tower, at the Hirschau, and beside the Kleinhesseloher See. Flaucher, located on the River Isar to the south of the city centre, is also well worth visiting (perhaps in combination with a bike ride along the river), as are Taxisgarten and Hirschgarten in the west of the city. *Weinstuben* (taverns), less numerous in the beer country of Bavaria than

The beer garden at the Chinese Tower in the English Garden

in other regions of Germany, serve wine by the glass rather than by the carafe or bottle, and provide meals.

Many Germans like to eat their main meal in the middle of the day, and generally prefer a lighter supper (*Abendbrot*, or 'evening bread') of cold meats and cheeses, possibly eaten with a salad, in the evening.

In a separate category is the *Konditorei* (a café-cum-pastry shop), the bourgeois fairyland where you can spend a whole afternoon reading the newspapers provided. This is the perfect place for a feast of pastry, ice cream, coffee, tea and fruit juices, with a good choice of wines. Most provide a limited selection of light snacks and salads.

WHAT TO EAT

Breakfast (Frühstück)
Germans start the day with a meal that is a bit more substantial than the typical 'Continental' breakfast. The distinctive touch is the selection of cold meats – including ham, salami and liver sausage *(Leberwurst)* – and cheese served with the bread. You will not find just one kind of bread, but a wide variety – brown (rye with caraway seeds), as well as rich black *(Pumpernickel)* and white. If you like boiled eggs, try *Eier im Glas* – two four-minute eggs served whole, already shelled, in a glass dish. And with it all comes tea, hot chocolate or coffee – stronger than the Anglo-American variety, but weaker than its French or Italian counterpart.

Soups and Starters
Bavarians specialise in excellent *Leberknödlsuppe*, a soup made with spicy dumplings of flour, breadcrumbs, beef

liver, onions, marjoram and garlic. *Kartoffelsuppe* contains potatoes, celery, leek and parsnip. Other popular soups are made with beans *(Bohnensuppe)* or lentils *(Linsensuppe)*, with pieces of sausage added to the mix.

If you prefer an hors d'oeuvre, try smoked calf's tongue served with a little horseradish sauce *(Kalbszüngerl mit Meerrettich)* or pork tongue boiled with a seasoning of juniper berries, bay leaves and peppercorns, accompanied by sauerkraut *(Schweinszüngerl im Kraut)*.

Bavarian Specialities

The pig and the calf dominate Bavarian main dishes, often in combination. Pork or veal can be either pot-roasted *(Kalbs-* or *Schweinebraten)* or grilled on a spit *(am Spieß)* to obtain a marvellous crackling skin. The Munich speciality is spit-roast *Schweinshaxn*, hock of pork, sold in halves or whole. Be careful when ordering – a half is a meal in itself. The ultimate delicious roast is *Spanferkel*, or suckling pig. For a change, sample the excellent game when in season – venison, hare, partridge and pheasant. Venison is often marinated until tender and served with a sauce of sweet raisins or redcurrants, or a purée of chestnuts. Try trout *(Forelle)* – this local freshwater fish is unbeatable if boiled absolutely fresh *(blau)* – or some whitefish *(Renke)*, usually fried. Bavarians also like their offal, one popular dish being *Saure Lüngerl* (chopped lung in vinegar sauce), which is best accompanied by a good glass of dry white wine.

Whether you've ordered *Saure Lüngerl* or *Schweinebraten*, your meal will often be accompanied by a large dumpling *(knödel)* or two, either of made of bread *(Semmelknödel)* or potato *(Kartoffelknödel)*; sautéed potatoes *(Bratkartoffeln)* may also be on the menu. Also available is the sweet-and-sour red cabbage, or *Blaukraut*, cooked with apples, raisins, onions, cloves and white vinegar. Plain *Sauerkraut* is often

Radishes *(Radi)* and carrots at the Viktualienmarkt

prepared in white wine with juniper berries or caraway seeds. Salads include cucumber salad *(Gurkensalat)*, a good white cabbage salad *(Weißkrautsalat),* or the excellent potato salad *(Kartoffelsalat).*

Snacks

You eat snacks *(Schmankerl)* at any time of day. Local people enjoy sausages of all kinds as a snack food. Pork and veal join forces in the *Weißwürste* (white sausages), flavoured with pepper, parsley and onions. The best establishments – and in this case we mean those most observant of traditional standards – never serve *Weißwürste* in the afternoon; they are then no longer considered fresh enough. *Bratwurst,* another sausage staple, is made of pork and grilled or sautéed. The best are the little ones from Nuremberg. You should also enjoy the spicy *Blutwurst* (blood sausage) or *Leberwurst* (liver sausage).

Also be on the look-out for a delicious snack with the misleading name of *Leberkäs*. Literally, this means 'liver-cheese', but it contains neither liver nor cheese, being rather a baked mixture of pork, bacon and beef, spiced with nutmeg, marjoram and onions, eaten hot or cold. Other great snacks include *Reiberdatschi*, or deep-fried potato pancakes; and *Obatzta*, a spicy mixture of creamy cheeses with chives, paprika, caraway seeds, salt and pepper, and thin slices of white radish *(Radi)*. Failing any of these, you will always be able to stimulate your thirst with the salty pretzels *(Brez'n)*.

Desserts

Kaiserschmarrn is a thick pancake sliced in strips, sprinkled with raisins and powdered sugar and served with plum compote or apple sauce. *Dampfnudel* is a steamed dumpling swimming in custard. Other delicious treats offered in Bavaria are *Schwarzwälder Kirschtorte*, the cherry cake from the Black Forest, and *Apfelstrudel*; *Zwetschgendatschi* (plum cake) is very popular during the summer and autumn.

Beer

Bavarians endorse the old saying that there's good beer and better beer, but no bad beer. Especially not in Bavaria. Protected by the oldest food law, Duke William's purity law *(Reinheitsgebot)* of 1516, which forbids the use of anything

---

Seasonal Drinking

It's not just at the Oktoberfest that the beer flows. In the third and fourth weeks before Easter, the so-called *Starkbierzeit* (Strong-beer Time), breweries promote their *Märzenbier* (March Ale). After Easter comes the *Maibockzeit*, when they push the strong dark stuff. In the summer, everybody's thirsty enough not to need too much prompting.

but water, barley and hops in brewing, Bavarian beer is still made today from natural products without any chemical additives.

If you like beer dark with a slightly sweet, malty flavour, order a *Dunkles*. This is not served as cold as *Helles*, the more popular light lager brew. Refreshing and well worth a try is *Weißbier*, a light, slightly cloudy brew made from wheat instead of barley and left to ferment in the bottle. The measure for beer is the *Maß*, which is one litre; half of this is *eine Halbe*, the usual measure if you order a beer in a restaurant. In beer gardens, most

Weißbier and Brez'n

beer is served in *Maßkrüge* (litre glasses). *Weißbier* is usually only served in half-litre measures, though in beer gardens it can be mixed with lemonade *(Limo)* to create *Weißbier* shandy, served by the litre and called a *Russenmaß*. Often the choice of cyclists who want to limit their alcohol intake, a *Radler* (cyclist) is a shandy made of *Helles* and *Limo*.

Wines

Bavaria itself stopped making good wine some centuries ago, though the restaurants in Munich offer an excellent array of Rhine and Mosel wines, mostly white and usually made from the astonishingly versatile Riesling grape. The best dry Rhine Rieslings to look out for come from the red-

Typical Bavarian fare: crispy roast pork, dumplings and beer

soiled vineyards of villages such as Nierstein and Nackenheim. Also popular and widely available in and around Munich are wines from the Franconia region, especially around Würzburg. Here Silvaner as well as Riesling grapes produce excellent dry whites, usually bottled in the distinctive green *bocksbeutel*. Excellent whites and reds from Baden will also be found on most wine lists.

Other Drinks

If you would rather be refreshed than stimulated, you'll find a wide assortment of fruit juices, the most common being *Johannisbeersaft* (red or black currant), *Apfelsaft* (apple), *Orangensaft* (orange) and *Traubensaft* (non-alcoholic grape).

To Help You Order

Waiter/waitress, please!	**Bedienung, bitte.**
Could I/we have a table?	**Ich hätte/Wir hätten gerne einen Tisch.**
The bill, please.	**zahlen, bitte.**
I would like ...	**Ich möchte gerne ...**

beer	**ein Bier**	mineral water	**Mineralwasser**
bread	**etwas Brot**	mustard	**etwas Senf**
butter	**etwas Butter**	pepper	**Pfeffer**
cheese	**Käse**	potatoes	**Kartoffeln**
coffee	**einen Kaffee**	salad	**Salat**
cream	**Sahne**	salt	**Salz**
dessert	**eine Nachspeise**	soup	**eine Suppe**
eggs	**Eier**	starter	**eine Vorspeise**
fish	**Fisch**	tea	**einen Tee**
ice cream	**Eiskrem**	wine	**Wein**
meat	**Fleisch**	vegetables	**Gemüse**
menu	**die Karte**		
milk	**Milch**		

... and Read the Menu

Apfel	apple	**Kartoffel-knödel**	potato dumpling
Blaukraut	red cabbage		
Blumenkohl	cauliflower	**Kraut**	cabbage
Braten	roast (pork or beef)	**Lachs**	salmon
		Lamm	lamb
Brat-kartoffeln	roast potatoes	**Nudeln**	noodles
		Reis	rice
Erdbeeren	strawberries	**Rindfleisch**	beef
Geräuchertes	smoked meat	**Rippchen**	smoked pork chops
Gurkensalat	cucumber salad		
Hähnchen	chicken (whole or half)	**Schinken**	ham
		Schweine-fleisch	pork
		Semmel-knödel	bread dumpling
Jäger-schnitzel	cutlet with mushroom sauce	**Wild**	game
		Wurst	sausage
Kalbfleisch	veal	**Zwiebeln**	onions

HANDY TRAVEL TIPS

An A–Z Summary of Practical Information

A

ACCOMMODATION (See also CAMPING, YOUTH HOSTELS and the list of Recommended Hotels starting on page 128)

The Munich Tourist Office (<www.munich-tourist.de>) publishes a free multilingual list of accommodation in the city, with full details of amenities and prices, available both online and from its offices in the city at Marienplatz and Hauptbahnhof. If you arrive at the station with no accommodation, the Tourist Information Office there (open Mon–Sat 9am–8pm in summer, 9.30am–6.30pm in winter) operates a hotel booking service for free, whereby part of the room rate must be paid in advance. For further assistance, tel: (089) 2339 6555, fax: (089) 2333 0233, and online booking through the website.

In addition to hotels, there are inns *(Gasthof)* and B&Bs *(Pension)*. The Tourist Office can arrange for accommodation in private homes – a nice way to get to know the local people. To rent rooms, apartments, flats and houses you can also try the website <www.statthotel.de>.

If you are touring Bavaria by car, look for *'Zimmer frei'* (room to rent) signs. A list of hotels and inns in Upper Bavaria is available from **Tourismusverband München-Oberbayern e.V.**, Radolfzeller Straße 13, 81243 München, tel: (089) 8292 180, <www.oberbayern-tourismus.de>.

Visitors should be aware that, in addition to the Oktoberfest, Munich hosts a variety of trade fairs and other events throughout the year, and so it's wise to check on dates with the tourist office and book rooms as far in advance as possible. Hotels raise their prices at busy times – by as much as 15 percent during the Oktoberfest.

I'd like a single/double room	**Ich möchte bitte ein Einzel-/ Doppelzimmer.**
with bath/shower	**mit Bad/Dusche**
What's the rate per night?	**Wieviel kostet es pro Nacht?**

AIRPORT *(Flughafen)* See also PUBLIC TRANSPORT

Munich Airport (<www.munich-airport.de>), about 30km (18 miles) east of the city centre, handles domestic and international flights. You will find banks, car rental desks, restaurants, coffee bars, news- and souvenir-stands, a post office, hairdresser and hotel reservation desk. For flight information, tel: (089) 9752 1313.

Getting into Munich. Taxis and suburban trains (S-Bahn) shuttle between the airport and the main railway station (Hauptbahnhof). The S-Bahn S8 runs every 20 minutes between the airport and Pasing via the city centre, and the S1 service approaches the city centre from the direction of Laim in the west, also every 20 minutes. Both stop at stations on the way. If you're getting off at Ostbahnhof or Marienplatz it's quicker to take the S8; for points west of Hauptbahnhof the S1 is the best option. Both services take about 40 minutes to reach Hauptbahnhof, and the journey costs €8.80 for a single ticket *(see page 121 for ticket details)*.

Where can I get a taxi?	**Wo finde ich ein Taxi?**
How much is it to the centre?	**Wieviel kostet es ins Zentrum?**

B

BICYCLE TOURS AND HIRE

With some 1,200km (800 miles) of cycle paths and its relatively flat terrain, Munich is renowned for being a cyclists' city. Most roads in the city have special cycle lanes, but as well as getting you around town a bike is great for exploring the banks of the River Isar and the Englisher Garten.

Information on tours can be obtained from Tourist Information or Mike's Bike Tours Munich, tel: (089) 2554 3988, <www.mikesbike-tours.com>, which also handles bike hire. Radius Bikes (inside the station opposite platform 32, tel: (089) 596113, fax: (089) 594714, <www.radiusmunich.com>) also rents out bikes from Apr–Oct.

BUDGETING FOR YOUR TRIP

To give you an idea of what to expect, here's a list of approximate prices in euros (€).

Airport transfer. S-Bahn lines 8 or 1 to main railway station (Hauptbahnhof): €8.80; taxi €50.

Car hire. This comes to about €75 per day for a VW Golf, €120 per day for a Mercedes C Class, including tax, location service charge, registration fee, collision damage waiver and theft protection.

Entertainment. Cinema €4.50–8, theatre €12–35, nightclub usually free.

Hotels (double room per night). Luxury class €250–400, first class €180–250, medium class €100–200, budget class €60–100. Boarding house €45–80.

Meals and drinks. Restaurants generally offer excellent value for money. A main course in a good Bavarian restaurant will be no more than €15 per head, while a gourmet meal prepared by a Michelin-starred chef won't be much more than €80 per head – much less expensive than prices in London, for example. A half-litre of beer will cost you €3 (more in a beer garden); a coffee €2–3.

Museums. No museum is free in Munich. Entrance costs between €1.50–€9.50 (eg: Stadtmuseum €4; Deutsches Museum €8.50; Pinakothek der Moderne €9.50). There are reduced family tickets.

MVV city transport. Day ticket: adults €5 (one zone), €10 (all zones); children €2.40 (all zones). Single ticket: €1.10 (short journey), €2.20 (one zone), each additional zone €2.20. Strip tickets: adults €10.50 (10-strip ticket), children €5.20 (5-strip ticket).

The **CityTourCard**, available from the city transport (MVG) sales points and ticket machines, selected hotels and station kiosks, allows unlimited travel on all public transport and offers discounts of up to 20 percent on entry to major city attractions. It costs €9.50 a day or €18 for three days for the single adult inner area version and is well worth it. *See page 121* for further details.

Taxis. €2.50, plus €1.45 per km within centre of Munich.

C

CAMPING

Four major campsites are situated within the city limits:

Langwieder See, Eschenrieder Straße 119, 81249 Munich, tel: (089) 864 1566, fax (089) 863 2342), <www.camping-langwieder-see.de>. Campsite idyllically located next to the lake of the same name, northwest of Munich along the Augsburg–Stuttgart motorway. Open all year.

München–Obermenzing, Lochhausener Straße 59, 81247 Munich, tel:(089) 811 2235, fax: (089) 814 4807, <www.campingplatz-muenchen.de>. Nice campsite to the northwest of Munich at Obermenzing (off the Augsburg-Stuttgart motorway). Open mid-March to end of October.

Campingplatz München-Thalkirchen, Zentralländstraße 49, 81379 Munich, tel: (089) 723 1707, fax: (089) 724 3177, <www.camping.muenchen.de>. Pleasantly situated campsite on the River Isar (the opposite bank to the zoo), with easy access to the city centre with the U-Bahn or No. 52 bus. Open mid-March to end of October.

The Tent (International Youthcamp Kapuzinerhölzl), In den Kirschen 30, 80992 Munich, tel: (089) 141 4300, fax: (089) 175090, <www.the-tent.com>. A campsite for young people in a pleasant park close to the Botanical Garden (reached by tram No. 17 from Hauptbahnhof). A tent large enough to accommodate 300 people is also available.

CAR HIRE *(Autovermietung)* See also DRIVING

You can arrange to rent a car immediately upon arrival at Munich's airport or main railway station (Hauptbahnhof). Otherwise enquire at your hotel or refer to the Yellow Pages of the telephone directory for addresses of leading firms. It's usually possible to have a car delivered to your hotel. Larger firms allow you to return cars to another European city for a small fee. Special weekend and weekly unlimited mileage rates are usually available. Many airlines offer fly/drive packages to Munich, which are good value if you want to leave the city for excursions.

To rent a car you'll need to have held a valid driver's licence for at least half a year; the minimum age is 19. If you do not pay by credit card you may have to pay a substantial cash deposit.

I'd like to rent a car	**Ich möchte bitte ein Auto mieten.**
tomorrow	**für morgen**
for one day/week	**für einen Tag/für eine Woche**
Please include full insurance.	**Bitte schließen Sie eine**
	Vollkaskoversicherung ab.

CLIMATE

Munich's climate can go to extremes, from the bitterest cold in winter to hot and either dry or muggy in summer. The dry, warm wind from the south, known as *Föhn,* can result in very clear, hot, dry conditions wonderful for visitors. Munich's average temperatures are given below.

	J	F	M	A	M	J	J	A	S	O	N	D
Daytime °C	1	3	9	14	18	21	23	23	20	13	7	2
Daytime °F	34	37	48	57	64	70	73	73	68	55	45	35

CLOTHING

During the winter months it can get very cold and windy, so you'll need a heavy coat and warm clothing. In summer you should bring plenty of lightweight garments, and a bathing suit if you want to sunbathe or take a dip. A light wrap can come in handy for cool summer evenings. It may rain in spring and summer, so be prepared with a raincoat or umbrella.

At better hotels and restaurants, more formal clothes are expected, but there are few places where a tie is obligatory.

CONSULATES *(Konsulat)*

Canada	Tal 29, tel: (089) 219 9570.
Ireland	Denninger Straße 15, tel: (089) 2080 5990.
South Africa	Sendlinger-Tor-Platz 5, tel: (089) 231 1630.
UK	Bürkleinstraße 10, tel: (089) 211090.
US	Königinstraße 5, tel: (089) 28880.

CRIME AND SAFETY See also EMERGENCIES and POLICE

Compared to many urban centres, Munich's crime rate is quite low. Nonetheless it's advisable to take all the normal precautions. Don't leave money or valuables in your car or hotel room; lock them in the hotel safe instead. If you are robbed, report the incident to the hotel receptionist and the nearest police station. The police will provide you with a certificate to present to your insurance company, or to your consulate if your passport has been stolen.

I want to report a theft.	**Ich möchte einen Diebstahl melden.**
My handbag/wallet/ passport has been stolen.	**Meine Handtasche/ Brieftasche/mein Pass ist gestohlen worden.**

CUSTOMS *(Zoll)* AND ENTRY REGULATIONS

For a stay of up to three months, a valid passport is sufficient for citizens of Australia, Canada, New Zealand, South Africa, and the United States. Citizens of European Union countries need only an identity card or passport to enter Germany.

As Germany is part of the European Union, the free exchange of non-duty-free goods for personal use is permitted between Germany, the UK and the Irish Republic (residents only). For non-European residents, and for goods bought duty-free within Europe and the EU, the restrictions on import into Germany are as follows: 200 cigarettes or 50 cigars or 250*g* tobacco, and 1*l* of spirits or 2*l* of wine (including fortified wines).

Restrictions for visitors from outside Europe on returning to their home country are as follows: **Australia**: 250*g* tobacco products and 1 litre of alcoholic beverages; **Canada**: 200 cigarettes and 50 cigars and 400*g* tobacco, 1.14*l* of liquor or wine or 8.5*l* of beer; **USA**: 200 cigarettes and 100 cigars and a reasonable amount of tobacco, 1 US quart of alcoholic beverages.

Currency restrictions. There are no restrictions on the import or export of euros or any other currency.

I've nothing to declare.	**Ich habe nichts zu verzollen.**
It's for my personal use.	**Es ist für meinen persönlichen Gebrauch.**

D

DRIVING IN MUNICH

To bring your car into Germany you will need: a national (or international for those coming from the US, Australia, or South Africa) driver's licence; car registration papers; a national identity car sticker; a red warning triangle in case of breakdown; and a first-aid kit.

Insurance. Third-party insurance is compulsory. For EU visitors, the international insurance certificate (Green Card) is no longer compulsory but is strongly recommended.

Seatbelts are obligatory for front-seat *and* back-seat passengers if the car is so equipped. If you don't wear them, insurance companies will reduce compensation in the event of an accident. Use of mobile phones while driving is forbidden and liable to a fine of €40.

Driving conditions. Traffic jams, a lack of parking space, pedestrian areas, and one-way streets all make driving in Munich a frustrating experience. It's far better to get around town using the public transport system, which is excellent – the tourist office provides a brochure listing points of interest and detailing how to get there by bus or underground. Bear in mind that bottlenecks form on major approach roads into Munich at the beginning and end of peak holiday periods.

Drive on the right, pass on the left. On the *Autobahn* (motorway, expressway), passing another vehicle on the right is prohibited; cars with trailers are not allowed to pass on certain stretches (watch for signs); and should police or emergency vehicles need to pass through a traffic jam *(Stau)*, cars in the right lane must keep close to the right, and those in the left lane close to the left, thereby opening a passageway down the middle. In the absence of traffic lights, or stop or give-way signs, vehicles coming from the right have priority at intersections, unless otherwise indicated. At roundabouts (traffic circles), approaching cars must give way to traffic already in the circle, unless otherwise indicated. Trams must be passed on the right and never at a stop (unless there's a traffic island).

At dusk, and in case of bad visibility, headlights or dipped headlights must be used; driving with parking lights only is forbidden, even in built-up areas.

Speed limits. The speed limit is 100 km/h (62 mph) on all open roads except for motorways and divided highways, where there's no limit unless otherwise indicated (the suggested maximum speed is 130 km/h, or 81 mph). In town, the limit is 50 km/h (31 mph), except on the Mittlerer Ring, the six-lane ring road system around the

Driving Licence	**Führerschein**
Car Registration Papers	**Kraftfahrzeugpapiere**
Green (insurance) Card	**Grüne Versicherungskarte**

city, where the limit is 60km/h (37mph). Cars towing trailers may not exceed 80 km/h (50 mph).

Road signs. Most road signs employed in Germany are international pictographs, but here are some written ones you might come across:

Einbahnstraße	One-way street
Einordnen	Get into lane
Fußgänger	Pedestrians
Kurzparkzone	Short-term parking
Links fahren	Keep left
Parken verboten	No parking
Umleitung	Detour
Vorsicht	Caution

Traffic police (see also POLICE) may confiscate the car keys of persons they consider unfit to drive. Drinking and driving is a very serious offence in Germany. The permissible level of alcohol in the blood is 0.8 per mille (millilitres), or about two glasses of beer. Be careful, too, to stay within speed limits; the police are getting ever stricter, and radar is used both inside and out of towns.

Breakdowns. In the event of a breakdown on the Autobahn and other important roads, use one of the emergency telephones located every second kilometre (the direction of the nearest one is indicated by a small arrow on the reflector poles at the roadside). Ask for

Where's the nearest car park?	**Wo ist der nächste Parkplatz?**
Full tank, please.	**Bitte volltanken.**
Super/lead-free/diesel	**Super/bleifreies Benzin/Diesel**
I've had a breakdown.	**Ich habe eine Panne.**
There's been an accident.	**Es ist ein Unfall passiert.**

Straßenwacht, run jointly by the two German automobile clubs ADAC and AvD. Assistance is free; towing and spare parts have to be paid for. For round-the-clock breakdown service, call (0180) 222 2222.

Fuel and oil *(Benzin; Öl).* Service stations are everywhere, many of them self-service. It's usual to tip attendants for any extra attention.

E

ELECTRICITY

Germany has 220-volt, 50-cycle AC. Plugs are the standard Continental type for which British and North American appliances need an adaptor.

EMERGENCIES (See also CONSULATES, DRIVING, MEDICAL CARE and POLICE)

Emergency telephone numbers:

Police:	**110**
Fire and emergency medical services:	**112**
Ambulance:	**19222**

If you don't speak German, try English, or ask the first person you see to help you call.

I need a doctor	**Ich brauche einen Arzt**
an ambulance	**einen Krankenwagen**
a hospital	**ein Krankenhaus**

G

GAY AND LESBIAN TRAVELLERS

Munich has an open atmosphere and is very accepting of all lifestyles. In particular, there is an area around the theatre district called Gärtnerplatz where there are many gay restaurants and clubs. *Our Munich* is a monthly gay and lesbian city magazine.

GETTING THERE (see also AIRPORT)

A good travel agent can give you up-to-date information on the wide range of fares, package holidays or short breaks currently available.

By air. Munich Airport is served by many European and about 90 intercontinental flights a day. However, the main airport for transatlantic flights is still Frankfurt, from where there are several flights a day to Munich. Average travel time from London to Munich is 1½ hours, from New York 9 hours.

By car. Munich can be reached by motorway (expressway) from nearly anywhere in Europe (Brussels–Munich 815 km/505 miles, Basel 394 km/244 miles, Hamburg 795 km/493 miles).

By coach. Tour operators in Germany and abroad offer coach tours to Munich all year round. Seats must be booked in advance. London to Munich direct takes approximately 24 hours.

By rail. It's now easy to travel from London to Munich by train in a day. Eurostar links London with Brussels in just 2½ hours, then high-speed Thalys trains link Brussels with Cologne in just 2½ hours more. Change in Cologne for the ICE connection to Munich. Or you can travel overnight from London to Munich with just one change – simply take an evening Eurostar from London to Paris or Brussels then an overnight sleeping-car or couchette from Paris to Munich. Reservations are obligatory on all services. Information on trains and reduced-price tickets is on page 122.

GUIDES AND TOURS

The tourist office will put you in touch with qualified guides and interpreters if you want a personally conducted tour or if you need linguistic assistance. City sightseeing tours by bus start from opposite the main entrance of the central railway station, in front of the Hertie department store. Enquire at the Tourist Information Office for details, or at Münchner Stadtrundfahrten, Arnulfstraße 8, tel: (089) 5502 8995, fax: (089) 5490 7570, <www.msr-muc.de>. There are various tours available, taking in city centre sights as well as peripheral attractions such as the Olympiapark, Schloss Nymphenburg and the Bavaria Film Studios.

Cycle tours of the city are also available *(see page 104)*, and walking tours. Stattreisen München (tel: 089-5440 4230, <www. stattreisen-muenchen.de>), Cityhopper Touren (tel: 089-272 1131) and Radius Tours (tel: 089-5502 9374) all offer special theme tours of the city.

We'd like an English-speaking guide.	**Wir möchten bitte einen englisch-sprechenden Führer.**
I'd like an English interpreter.	**Ich möchte bitte einen Dolmetscher.**

H

HEALTH AND MEDICAL CARE See also EMERGENCIES

If you already have private medical insurance, find out whether or not you are covered for treatment in Germany. Visitors who are not covered can take out a short-term holiday policy before setting out.

Citizens of European Union countries are eligible for free medical treatment and should obtain the European Health Insurance Card from their Health and Social Security office or post office prior to their departure. However, it is still advisable to take out holiday insurance; a reputable policy will provide far more comprehensive coverage in the case of serious illness or accident.

In an emergency call for an ambulance (**19 222**). If you require medical attention it is possible to contact the appropriate consulate for a list of English-speaking doctors and dentists.

| Where's the nearest (all-night) pharmacy? | **Wo ist die nächste Apotheke (mit Nachtdienst)?** |

Pharmacies are open during normal shopping hours. At night, on Sundays and on holidays, all pharmacies display the address of the nearest one open. International pharmacies are located close to the main station: Inter Apotheke, Elisenstraße 5, tel: (089) 595444, <www. inter-apotheke.de>; Schützenapotheke, Schützenstraße 5/Bayerstraße 4, tel: (089) 557661, <www. schuetzenapotheke.com/englisch>.

It is perfectly safe to drink the tap water in Germany; only rarely will you see the sign 'Kein Trinkwasser' (which means 'not drinking water', usually at public squares and in trains).

HOLIDAYS *(Feiertage)*

On public holidays, shops, banks, offices and many restaurants are closed. If a holiday falls on a Thursday, it may turn into a long weekend. On 24 and 31 December, shops are open until midday.

1 January	**Neujahr**	New Year's Day
6 January	**Heilige Drei Könige**	Epiphany
1 May	**Tag der Arbeit**	Labour Day
15 August	**Mariä Himmelfahrt**	Assumption Day
3 October	**Nationalfeiertag**	Reunification Day
1 November	**Allerheiligen**	All Saints' Day
25, 26 December	**Weihnachten**	Christmas
Movable dates:	**Karfreitag**	Good Friday
	Ostermontag	Easter Monday
	Christi Himmelfahrt	Ascension Day
	Pfingstmontag	Whit Monday
	Fronleichnam	Corpus Christi

I

INTERNET CAFES

Many hotels offer e-mail facilities to their guests. In addition, there are several Internet cafés in the city, such as: Internetcafé Altheimer Eck, Altheimer Eck 12 (open daily 11am–1am); Internet-Point am Marienplatz (U-Bahn Viktualienmarkt exit; open daily 24 hours), Times Square Online Bistro, Bayerstraße 10a (near the station; open daily 7.30–1am); EasyEverything, Bahnhofsplatz 1 (open daily 24 hours); Coffee Fellows Schwabing, Leopoldstraße 70 (Schwabing; open Mon–Thur 7.30am– midnight, Fri 7.30–1am, Sat 8.30–1am, Sun 9am–midnight).

L

LANGUAGE

About one-third of the Munich population speaks a form of Bavarian dialect. Real Bavarian is difficult to understand, even for the many northern Germans who live in Munich, but Bavarians can often be persuaded to speak something closer to standard German. English is widely understood and spoken, and most of the larger shops have English-speaking staff, but don't take it for granted.

| Do you speak English? | **Sprechen Sie Englisch?** |

LOST PROPERTY

Munich's general lost-property office, Fundbüro der Stadtverwaltung, is at Oetztaler Straße 17, tel: (089) 2339 6045. You should contact them if you've left belongings on the bus or tram. If you've lost something on the U-Bahn, contact the *MVG Infopoint* at the main railway station (Hauptbahnhof, tel: 089-2191 3240). For property lost on trains (including S-Bahn), contact the *Fundbüro* at the main station (tel: 089-1308 6664) if it is within three days of the loss; otherwise, contact the main lost-property offices of the Bundesbahn, at Landsberger Straße 472, tel: (089) 1308 5859.

I've lost my wallet/my bag/my passport.	**Ich habe meine Brieftasche/meine Tasche/ meinen Pass verloren.**

M

MEDIA

Newspapers and magazines *(Zeitungen; Zeitschriften)*. Major British, American and Continental newspapers and magazines are on sale at newsstands in the city centre, as well as at larger hotels, the main railway station and the airport. *In München* is a guide in German to upcoming events, published every two weeks and available from the tourist office, hotels and newsstands. *Munich Found* (<www. munichfound.de>), Munich's monthly English-language magazine with valuable tips on culture and entertainment, and much else besides, is available from kiosks and bookshops. There are two English bookshops in Munich, both in Schellingstraße near the university.

Have you any English-language newspapers?	**Haben Sie Zeitungen in englischer Sprache?**

Radio and TV *(Radio; Fernsehen)*. You can easily pick up the BBC World Service. As for television, there are two commercial-free national channels – ARD and ZDF, plus a regional station BR *(Bayerischer Rundfunk)*. There are also several private and cable stations, while most hotels will also have satellite television, so you should also be able to watch CNN and BBC World.

MONEY MATTERS See also CUSTOMS AND ENTRY REGULATIONS

Currency. Germany's monetary unit is the euro (€), which is divided into 100 cents. Coins: 1, 2, 5, 10, 20 and 50 cents, and €1 and 2. Notes: € 5, 10, 20, 50, 100, 200 and 500.

ATMS. These are located throughout the city. Many offer cash withdrawal for Visa, MasterCard, American Express, Cirrus or Plus cards. Be sure to know your PIN for cash withdrawals on debit/credit cards.

Banks and currency exchange. Foreign currency can be changed at ordinary banks *(Bank)*, savings banks *(Sparkasse)* and currency exchange offices *(Wechselstube)*. It can also be changed at hotels, travel agencies and Munich's central post office, but rates are not as good. Money can be changed at the ReiseBank in the main railway station from 7am to 10pm every day, or at the main post office Mon–Fri 7.30am–8pm, Sat 9am–4pm. Always take your passport with you to change money or travellers' cheques.

Credit cards are accepted in most major hotels and many restaurants, shops and major service stations.

Travellers' cheques can be changed at all banks, but cannot be used to make purchases in shops.

Can I pay with this credit card?	**Kann ich mit dieser Kreditkarte bezahlen?**
I want to change some pounds/dollars.	**Ich möchte Pfund/Dollar wechseln.**
Can you cash a traveller's cheque?	**Können Sie einen Reisescheck einlösen?**
Where's the nearest bank/currency exchange office?	**Wo ist die nächste Bank/Wechselstube?**
Is there a cash machine near here?	**Gibt es hier einen Geldautomaten?**
How much is that?	**Wieviel kostet das?**

O

OPENING HOURS See also HOLIDAYS

Banks are usually open from 8.30am–12.30pm and 1.30–3.30pm, Monday to Friday (Thursday until 5.30pm). Some bigger banks in the city centre remain open during lunch hour. Banks at the airport operate daily from about 7am until around 9pm. Transactions can also be made at the central railway station daily from 6am–11pm.

Museum hours vary, but are usually from 9.30am–5pm or 6pm. Most museums close on Mondays.

Restaurants in the city centre often stay open all day. Breakfast is until 10am, lunch noon–2.30pm and dinner 6–11pm.

Shops are generally open from 8.30 or 9am–8pm, Monday to Friday, and till 4pm (some till 12.30pm) on Saturdays. Shops outside the city centre usually close between 1 and 3pm.

P

PHOTOGRAPHY

All makes of film are easily found and can be developed overnight or even within an hour. Digital accessories and video cassettes are also widely available, though you must make sure they are compatible with your equipment back home.

POLICE *(Polizei)* See also EMERGENCIES

Germany's police wear green uniforms. You'll see them on white motorcycles or in green-and-white cars. Street parking in towns is supervised by police wardens in dark-blue uniforms. If you are fined, they have the right to ask you to pay on the spot.

Where's the nearest police station?	**Wo ist die nächste Polizeistation?**

The police emergency number is **110**; the Fire Department/Ambulance Service is **112**. Munich's central police station *(Polizeipräsidium)* is at Ettstraße 2, close to the Frauenkirche.

POST OFFICES

Munich's central post office is opposite the main railway station (Hauptbahnhof). It is open Monday–Friday 7.30am–8pm, Saturday 9am–4pm. Most post offices are open from 8am–6 or 7pm Monday to Friday (till noon on Saturdays). They also handle telegrams and telephone calls.

Postboxes are painted yellow with a black post-horn. Stamps can be purchased at yellow vending machines near postboxes and at some tobacconists and stationers.

Poste restante (general delivery). This service is taken care of by Munich's central post office: If you have mail addressed to you c/o Hauptpostlagernd, it will arrive at the central post office. Always be sure to take your passport or identity card when you go to collect your mail.

Where's the nearest post office?	**Wo ist das nächste Postamt?**
A stamp for this	**Eine Briefmarke für diesen**
letter/ postcard, please.	**Brief/diese Karte, bitte.**
express (special delivery)	**per Eilboten**
registered	**per Einschreiben**

PUBLIC TRANSPORT

Munich is served by a highly efficient network of buses, trams, U-Bahn (underground railway) and S-Bahn (suburban railway, all coordinated by the MVV (Munich Transport and Tariff Association, <www.mvv-muenchen.de>). The U- and S-Bahn serve the city centre, while the S-Bahn goes out to suburbs and the surrounding countryside. All forms of public transport operate from about 5am to 1am daily, with special night services till around 4am. Free maps and information are available at the tourist offices. The MVV runs on an honour system. Your ticket is not checked as you get on, but instead there are frequent random checks. Fines of €50 are automatic if you can't produce a correct ticket immediately.

Tickets, interchangeable between U-Bahn, S-Bahn, buses and trams, entitle you to free transfers for up to 3 hours in one zone, 2 hours in two and more zones, so long as you travel in the same direction. Buy your tickets from the big blue vending machines at U- and S-Bahn stations (or on buses and at tram stops, hotels, tobacconists, newsagents and stationers that display a white 'K'). Vending machines are marked *Einzelfahrkarte* (single ticket) or *Streifenenkarte* (strip ticket). The strip tickets work out cheaper if you intend to make several trips. Be sure to cancel tickets in the blue cancelling machines positioned at platform entrances and in buses and trams; if you have a strip ticket you need to cancel **two** strips per zone travelled (children cancel only one strip per zone), unless you travel only one stop by U- or S-Bahn or two stops by bus or tram – then one strip is sufficient.

From the airport. If, during your stay you're only going to be needing public transport in the central area, it's best for this journey to buy a 10-strip ticket *(Streifenkarte)* for €10.50. Cancelling eight of the 10 strips is enough to get you through the four zones to the city centre, so the journey effectively costs €8.40.

CityTourCard. The MVV also has a day ticket *(see page 105)* and a 3-day inner district ticket, both available as partner tickets for two people. But the best deal for short-stay visitors is probably the CityTourCard, which provides unlimited use of the network as well as reductions for many of the city's major museums and attractions. The card is available from MVV ticket counters and automatic ticket machines, and prices are as follows (2007):

> 1-Day CityTourCard, inner area €9.50
>
> 3-Day CityTourCard, inner area €18

What's the fare to ... ?	**Wieviel kostet es nach ...?**
Where is the nearest bus stop?	**Wo ist die nächste Bushaltestelle?**
When's the next bus to ...?	**Wann geht der nächste Bus nach ...?**
I want a ticket to ... single/return	**Ich will eine Fahrkarte nach ... einfache Karte/Rückfahrkarte**
Will you tell me when to get off?	**Könnten Sie mir bitte sagen, wann ich aussteigen muss.**

Taxis. Munich taxis, usually Mercedes, are cream in colour. Catch one at a taxi stand or hail a taxi in the street.

Intercity bus services. Rural areas are served by local companies for the Munich Transport Association. Buses of the Deutsche Touring Gesellschaft (DTG) connect Munich to other European cities (ticket center at Hirtenstraße 4, tel: (089) 8898 9513, <www.deutsche-touring.de>). In Munich, the bus terminal is in Arnulfstraße, in front of Starnberger Bahnhof (at the north side of the main railway station).

Trains. Deutsche Bahn (DB, <www.bahn.de>) trains are comfortable and fast, as well as punctual. EC (Euro City) are international trains; IC (Inter City) and ICE (Inter City Express) are long-distance national trains. The ICE trains are very fast, reaching speeds of up to 280 kph (174 mph), and feature restaurants and aircraft-like video screens on some seats. IR (InterRegio) trains run every hour between major cities, and RE (Regional Express) are local trains.

Reduced price offers and bargain tickets are available, particularly for small groups and weekend travel. Eurail pass rail tickets cover Western Europe, are only available to those living outside Europe and must be bought before you arrive in Europe; Euro Domino passes allow unlimited travel in Germany for any three to eight days within one month; the Bahncard – suitable for frequent travellers in Germany – allows discounts of 50 percent off the regular fare for all train journeys in the country over a one-year period. Detailed information is available in the UK from Deutsche Bahn UK (<www.deutsche-bahn.co.uk>, tel: 08702 43 53 63). For further details, ask at travel agencies, German National Tourist offices in your home country, or DB railway offices.

Hitchhiking. This is forbidden only on the Autobahn. However, if you try thumbing a lift, you may have a long wait.

Car-share groups. Some associations arrange intercity trips *(Mitfahrgelegenheiten)*; try the following addresses in Munich:

Mitfahrzentrale, Lämmerstraße 6, tel: (089) 19440; fax: (089) 594564, <www.mitfahrzentralen.de>

Citynetz Mitfahrzentrale München, Adalbertstraße 6, tel: (089) 19444; fax: (089) 3304 0068, <www.citynetz-mitfahrzentrale.de>

There are fixed-price tickets for the journeys, according to the distance, and insurance is also available.

R

RELIGION

Almost half of the Munich population is Roman Catholic and about one-third Protestant. There is also a large Jewish community.

Several church services are held in English for different denominations, such as: St. Bonifaz, Karlstraße; Kreuzkirche, Kreuzstraße (Roman Catholic) and Seybothstraße 4 (Anglican- Episcopal). For links to these and other churches, visit the website of Munich's English-language information magazine *Munich Found*: <www.munichfound.de>.

T

TELEPHONE

The dialling code for Germany is 49. The dialling code for Munich from outside the city is 089. For international calls from Munich, dial 00 before the country code (44 for UK, 1 for US), then the area code and number of your destination. Avoid placing calls through your hotel, as the fee is likely to be considerably higher than in a phone booth. Telephone booths can be identified by their distinctive pink-coloured tops and receivers. Communications within Germany and to neighbouring countries are cheaper after 6pm weekdays and all day Saturdays, Sundays and national holidays. Telephone cards for €5, €10 or €20 can be purchased at the post office.

Enquiries: domestic, tel: 11833; international, tel: 11834.

TIME ZONES

Germany follows Central European Time (GMT + 1). In summer, the clock is put one hour ahead (GMT + 2):

New York	London	**Munich**	Jo'burg	Sydney	Auckland
6am	11am	**noon**	noon	8pm	10pm

What time is it, please?	**Wie spät ist es, bitte?**

TIPPING

Since a service charge is normally included in hotel and restaurant bills, tipping is not obligatory, but is widely practised. It's appropriate to give something extra to porters and cloakroom attendants for their services. Below are some suggestions as to how much to leave.

Porter, per bag	€0.80
Maid, per week	€2.50–5
Lavatory attendant	€0.15–0.25
Waiter	optional (round off)
Taxi driver	round off
Hairdresser/Barber	10–15 percent
Tour guide	10 percent

TOILETS

Public toilets are easily found: museums, all restaurants, bars, cafés, large stores, airports and railway stations provide facilities. If there's an attendant, and hand towels and soap are offered, you should leave a small tip. Always have some small change ready in case the door has a coin-operated latch. Toilets may be labelled with symbols of a man or a woman or the initials *W. C.* Otherwise *Herren* (Gentlemen) and *Damen* (Ladies) or a double zero (00) sign are indicated.

Where are the toilets?	**Wo sind die Toiletten?**

TOURIST INFORMATION

The German National Tourist Board – Deutsche Zentrale für Tourismus (DZT) – can inform you about when to go, where to stay and what to see in Munich: DZT, Beethovenstraße 69, D-60325 Frankfurt am Main, tel: (069) 974 640, fax: (069) 751 903, <www.germany-tourism.de>.

The German National Tourist Board also maintains offices in many countries throughout the world, including:

Canada: 480 University Avenue, Suite 1410, Toronto, Ontario M5G 1V2, tel: (416) 968-1685, toll-free: (877) 315 6237, fax: (416) 968-0562; <www.cometogermany.com>.

UK: P.O. Box 2695, London W1A 3TN, tel: 020-7317 0908, fax: 020-7317 0917, <www.germany-tourism.co.uk>

US: 122 East 42nd Street, 20th Floor, Suite 2000, New York, NY 10168, tel: (212) 661-7200, fax: (212) 6617174, <www.cometogermany.com>.

The Munich Tourist Board (<www.munich-tourist.de>) maintains two Tourist Offices in the city, located at Hauptbahnhof (the

main railway station), Bahnhofsplatz 2 (open Mon–Sat 9am–8pm
in summer, 9.30am–6.30pm in winter), and in the Town Hall,
Marienplatz (open Mon–Fri 10am–8pm, Sat 10am–4pm). Written,
phone or e-mail enquiries should be directed to: Fremden-
verkehrsamt München, 80313 Munich, tel: (089) 2339 6500, fax:
(089) 2333 0233; e-mail: <tourismus@muenchen.de>.

The Tourist Offices offer a hotel booking service for a small fee.
The official *Monatsprogramm* of events is on sale there. You can
also listen to recorded information in English for museums and galleries, tel: (089) 2333 0070.

For information about Bavaria, contact the Munich–Upper
Bavaria Tourist Association at the following address: Tourismusverband München-Oberbayern e.V., Radolfzeller Straße 15, tel:
(089) 8292 180, <www.oberbayern-tourismus.de>.

TRAVELLERS WITH DISABILITIES

Munich is a very accessible city, with most large hotels, museums
and public transport equipped with ramps, lifts and special access.
It's advisable to check at smaller places before you go.

City guides are available to accompany visitors with disabilities;
call (089) 356 8808 Tuesday and Thursday 6 to 8pm.

Munich's central post office, opposite the station, has write-read
phones available for the hearing-impaired.

W

WEBSITES

A great deal of information about Munich can be obtained from the
Internet. Some useful addresses include:

<www.munich-tourist.de> (the English-language site of the
Munich Tourist Board).

<www.munichfound.de> (the website of *Munich Found*, the city's
monthly English-language information magazine).

<www.in-muenchen.de> (website of *In-München* magazine).

<www.deutsches-museum.de> (Deutsches Museum site).

<www.pinakothek.de> (Munich's three pinakotheks).

<www.munich-online.de> (German-language site that can be useful even if you don't speak German, as it contains information about forthcoming events, etc).

<www.messe-muenchen.de> (trade fair site).

<www.oktoberfest.de> (official Oktoberfest site).

<www.tollwood.de> (Tollwood Festival site).

<www.staatsoper.de> (the Bavarian National Opera).

Y

YOUTH HOSTELS

If you're planning to make extensive use of youth hostels during your stay in Munich, obtain an international membership card from your national youth hostel association. For full information about hostels in Germany, contact the German Youth Hostel Association (Deutsches Jugendherbergswerk – DJH, <www.djh.de>. The following youth hostels are located in and around Munich:

Jugendherberge Burg Schwaneck, Burgweg 4–6, 82049 Pullach im Isartal, tel: (089) 7448 6670, fax: (089) 7448 6680, <www.burgschwaneck.de>. Located in a castle to the south of Munich, overlooking the picturesque Isar Valley.

Jugendherberge München-Thalkirchen, Miesingstraße 4, 81379 Munich, tel: 723 6550, fax: 724 2567, <www.djh.de>. Modern youth hostel by the river with easy access to the centre.

Jugendherberge München-Neuhausen, Wendl-Dietrich-Straße 20, 80634 Munich, tel: (089) 131156, fax: (089) 167 8745, <www.djh.de>. Pleasant youth hostel in the district of Neuhausen.

Other hostels that don't require a membership card include those listed on pages 131 (Easy Palace City Hostel) and 134 (Haus International).

Recommended Hotels

The following selection of recommended hotels is arranged under headings according to geographical location: Innenstadt (for the Old City centre); the Station and the West (for the station and Oktoberfest); Isar and the East (for locations along or near the river and quick access to the trade fair grounds at Riem); and Schwabing and the North (including spots near the Englischer Garten and Olympiapark).

There are hotel booking facilities at the main tourist information offices in Munich (see Accommodation on page 103, and Tourist Information Offices on page 125). Because Munich is an important conference and trade fair centre, it's vital to book good and early; during the Oktoberfest, which lasts for 16 days up to the first Sunday in October, rooms are very hard to come by.

The symbols below are a guide to the price of a standard double room with bathroom. Breakfast may be extra. The so-called hotels 'garni' supply breakfast only, no restaurant meals. All prices are inclusive of service and tax.

€€€€	Above 250 euros
€€€	180–250 euros
€€	100–180 euros
€	Below 100 euros

INNENSTADT (CITY CENTRE)

Advokat €€–€€€ *Baaderstraße 1, 80469 Munich, tel: (089) 216310, fax: (089) 216 3190, <www.hotel-advokat.de>*. Stylish hotel with modern interior, located in the fashionable Gärtnerplatz district, just five minutes' walk from Marienplatz. Great breakfast. 50 rooms.

Asam Stadthotel €€ *Josephspitalstraße 3, 80331 Munich, tel: (089) 2309 700, fax: (089) 2309 7097, <www.hotel-asam.de>*. Pleasant family-run hotel in a converted five-storey townhouse just five minutes' walk from Marienplatz. The large and airy rooms are luxuriously appointed and have beautiful granite bathrooms. Rear bedrooms look over pleasant garden. 25 rooms.

Bayerischer Hof & Palais Montgelas €€€€ *Promenadeplatz 2–6, 80333 Munich, tel: (089) 21200, fax: (089) 2120 906, <www.bayerischerhof.de>.* Luxury hotel in the heart of Munich built in 1841 on the orders of Ludwig I and now also occupying the neighbouring Palais Montgelas. You can take your pick from five different elegant styles of room, and facilities include bars and restaurants, roof-top garden, swimming pool, sauna and shops. 395 rooms.

Hotel An der Oper €€€ *Falkenturmstraße 10, 80331 Munich, tel: (089) 2900 270, fax: 2900 2729, <www.hotelanderoper.de>.* Five-floor hotel built in 1969, just off Maximilianstraße. Its elegantly designed, comfortable rooms and superb location make this hotel cheap at the price. 69 rooms.

Hotel Exquisit €€€ *Pettenkoferstraße 3, 80336 Munich, tel: (089) 5519 900; fax: (089) 5519 9499, <www.augustiner-restaurant. com>.* Comfortable hotel located close to Sendlinger Tor, a 10-minute walk from Marienplatz. Good buffet breakfast. Sauna, solarium, garden terrace. 50 rooms.

Kempinski Hotel Vier Jahreszeiten München €€€€ *Maximilianstraße 17, 80539 Munich, tel: (089) 21250, fax: (089) 2125 2777, <www.kempinski-vierjahreszeiten.com>.* Munich's most distinctive hotel, part of the fabric of elegant Maximilianstraße. Its rooms and suites are sumptuously appointed, and the large bathrooms are equipped with all sorts of special treats. Facilities include a restaurant, bar, pool, sauna and solarium. 308 rooms and suites.

Mandarin Oriental €€€€ *Neuturmstraße 1, 80331 Munich, tel: (089) 290980, fax: (089) 222539, <www.mandarinoriental.com>.* Small but very elegant hotel in a wedge-shaped neoclassical building around the corner from the Hofbräuhaus. It is known for having the most spacious rooms in the city, each one fitted out with hand-made furnishings. There's a rooftop terrace with heated swimming pool and spectacular 360° city views. The sweeping marble staircase in the lobby leads up to the acclaimed Mark's Corner restaurant, a gourmet's delight. 53 rooms, 20 suites.

Hotel Olympic €€–€€€ *Hans-Sachs-Straße 4, 80469 Munich, tel: (089) 231890, fax: (089) 2318 9199, <www.hotel-olympic. de>*. Tastefully converted Victorian villa situated on a pretty street in the Glockenbach district between Gärtnerplatz and Sendlingertor. Most rooms look out onto a peaceful courtyard. Friendly service, excellent breakfast. 38 rooms.

Platzl Hotel €€–€€€ *Sparkassenstraße 10, 80331 Munich, tel: (089) 237030; fax: (089) 2370 3800*. On the site of an old mill dating from the 16th century, the Platzl has tastefully appointed rooms, most in contemporary style but with the option of the 'Bavarian Suite'. The 'Moorish Kiosk' recreation area has state of the art fitness and wellness facilities. 167 rooms.

Schlicker 'Zum goldenen Löwen' €€–€€€ *Tal 8, 80331 Munich, tel: (089) 242 8870; fax: (089) 296059, <www.hotel-schlicker.de>*. Comfortable, family-run hotel garni in a building dating back to the 16th century, just steps away from Marienplatz and around the corner from the Viktualienmarkt. 68 rooms.

THE STATION AND THE WEST

Alfa € *Hirtenstraße 22, 80335 Munich, tel: (089) 5459 530, fax: (089) 5459 53299, <www.hotel-alfa.de>*. Hotel garni conveniently situated near the station, but in a quiet side-street location. Garage and other parking available. 76 rooms.

Arabella Sheraton Westpark €€–€€€€ *Garmischer Straße 2, 80339 Munich, tel: (089) 51960, fax: (089) 5196 801, <www.arabellasheraton.com>*. Modern hotel overlooking the idyllic Westpark. Landscaped bathing complex, with swimming pool, whirlpool, sauna, steam bath, solarium and bar; restaurant and cocktail bar; conference facilities. 258 rooms.

City Hotel €–€€€ *Schillerstraße 3a, 80336 Munich, tel: (089) 515 5390, fax: (089) 550 3665, <www.city-hotel-muenchen.de>*. Six-storey hotel close to the station that combines coziness with a modern design. All bedrooms with ensuite. Buffet breakfast. 71 rooms.

Deutsches Theater €€ *Landwehrstraße 18, 80336 Munich, tel: (089) 5458 525, fax: (089) 5458 5261, <www.hoteldeutschestheater. de>*. Relaxed hotel garni in a central location. All rooms are decorated with Laura Ashley-style fabrics. Lobby bar open 24 hours a day; good breakfast buffet. 27 rooms.

Easy Palace City Hostel € *Mozartstraße 4, 80336 Munich, tel: (089) 5587 9755, fax: (089) 5587 9797, <www.easypalace.com>*. Great value accommodation between the station and Stachus; clean rooms and dorms, friendly service.

Eden-Hotel-Wolff €€–€€€€ *Arnulfstraße 4–8, 80335 Munich, tel: (089) 551150, fax: (089) 5511 5555, <www.ehw.de>*. The plain exterior of this hotel opposite the station belies the class of the establishment, from the excellent service to the individual, modern décor of each room. Modern wellness centre including gym and sauna; conference facilities. 214 rooms and suites.

Europäischer Hof €–€€ *Bayerstraße 31, 80335 Munich, tel: (089) 551510, fax (089) 5515 1444, <www.heh.de>*. Comfortable, family-run hotel opposite the station, with various classes of rooms available. Paintings in the rooms and corridors provide a personal touch. 145 rooms.

Garagen-Hotel €–€€ *Lindwurmstraße 20–30, 80337 Munich, tel: (089) 5442 440, fax: (089) 5442 4499, <www.garagen-hotel.de>*. Peaceful family-style hotel garni in a convenient location for the Oktoberfest. Parking available. 24 rooms.

Hahn Hotel €–€€ *Landsberger Straße 117, 80339 Munich, tel: (089) 5108 9590, fax: (089) 5108 959109, <www.hotel-hahn.de>*. Family-run hotel garni decorated in the Bavarian-baroque style, with friendly service. Parking and bar. 40 rooms.

InterCityHotel München €€ *Bayerstraße 10; 80335 Munich, tel: (089) 444440, fax: (089) 4444 4599, <www.intercityhotel.de>.* This is Munich's original station hotel, once an art nouveau show-piece but now completely redone in contemporary style. Very handy for the station; pleasant rooms all with en-suite; restaurant and bar. 198 rooms.

Mercure München City Center €€ *Senefelderstaße 9, 80336 Munich, tel: (089) 551320, fax: (089) 596444, <www.mercure. com>.* Newly renovated hotel just 300m from the station. Restaurant with regional and international cuisine, beer garden; conference rooms. 167 rooms.

Hotel Mirabell €–€€€ *Landwehrstraße 42 (entrance Goethe-straße), 80336 Munich, tel: (089) 549 1740, fax: (089) 550 3701, <www.hotelmirabell.de>.* Good value family-run hotel garni next to the station. 68 modern rooms.

Nymphenburg €€ *Nymphenburger Straße 141, 80636 Munich, tel: (089) 121 5970, fax: (089) 182540, <www.hotel-nymphenburg.de>.* Good service in this quiet hotel situated in the district of Neuhausen, not far from Schloss Nymphenburg. Pleasant, individually-designed rooms, most facing away from the street. 44 rooms.

Uhland Garni €€ *Uhlandstraße 1, 80336 Munich, tel: (089) 543350, fax: (089) 5433 5250, <www.hotel-uhland.de>.* Family-run hotel garni in a *Jugendstil* villa adjacent to the Theresienwiese. A good choice for families as many units contain bunk beds for children. Continental and traditional Bavarian breakfast included. 27 rooms.

ISAR AND THE EAST

Admiral München €€€ *Kohlstraße 9, 80469 Munich, tel: (089) 216350; fax: (089) 293674, <www.hotel-admiral.de>.* Hotel garni in a tranquil location on the west bank of the Isar near the Deutsches Museum, a short walking distance from the central city sights. Some of the elegantly furnished rooms have a balcony overlooking the lovely garden. Bar available. Excellent breakfast buffet. 33 rooms.

Apart Hotels & Residences €€–€€€ *Brudermühlstraße 33, 81371 Munich, tel: (089) 724940, fax: (089) 7249 4700, <www. apart-muenchen.de>.* Modern hotel to the southwest of the centre close to the Isar and the Flaucher beer garden. All rooms equipped with a kitchen; also a fitness centre with sauna and solarium. Italian restaurant, bar and massive roof-deck with superb view. 98 rooms.

Arabella Sheraton Grand Hotel €€€€ *Arabellastraße 6, 81925 Munich, tel: (089) 92640, fax: (089) 9264 8699, <www. arabellasheraton.com>.* This is the largest hotel in Munich, a 22-storey building located in the Bogenhausen district of the city. It has a swimming pool on the top floor, plus a series of whirlpools, saunas and steam rooms. Conference facilities. 643 rooms.

Hotel Domus €€ *St-Anna-Straße 31, 80538 Munich, tel: (089) 217 7730, fax: (089) 228 5359, <www.domus-hotel.de>.* Modern five-storey hotel garni in the peaceful district of Lehel between Maximilianstraße and the Englisher Garten, and close to the Isar. Tastefully furnished rooms, all with bathrooms with shower-tub combinations. Good breakfast buffet. 45 rooms.

Hilton Munich City €€–€€€€ *Rosenheimer Straße 15, 81667 Munich, tel: (089) 48040, fax: (089) 4804 4804, <www.hilton.com>.* In the district of Haidhausen near the Gasteig cultural centre, and just a short walk from the Isar and the Deutsches Museum. Facilities include two restaurants serving German and regional specialities, the Caffè Cino and a fully-equipped business centre. 480 rooms.

Holiday Inn Munich City Centre €€–€€€€ *Hochstraße 3, 81669 Munich, tel: (089) 48030, fax: (089) 448 7170, <www.holidayinn. de>.* Opposite the Gasteig cultural centre, above the Isar, this large, refurbished hotel has elegant modern décor and all imaginable facilities, including swimming pool, sauna and steam bath. Business centre and extensive conference facilities. 582 rooms.

Prinzregent €€€ *Ismaninger Straße 42–44, 81675 Munich, tel: (089) 416050, fax: (089) 4160 5466, <www.prinzregent.de>.* Exclusive, traditionally decorated, Bavarian-style hotel garni in quiet location close to the Friedensengel ('Angel of Peace') above the Isar. Facilities include sauna and bar, and breakfast can be enjoyed either in the rustic-style breakfast room or the conservatory. 65 rooms.

SCHWABING AND THE NORTH

Biederstein €€ *Keferstraße 18, 80802 Munich, tel: (089) 389 9970, fax: (089) 389 997389, <www.hotelbiederstein.de>.* Idyllic location at the edge of the Englischer Garten, many rooms with private balcony. Breakfast on the terrace in summer. 34 rooms.

Gästehaus Englischer Garten €–€€ *Liebergesellstraße 8, 80802 Munich, tel: (089) 3839 410, fax: (089) 3839 4133, <www.hotel englischergarten.de>.* Delightful old villa in a tranquil location by the Englischer Garten. Nicely furnished rooms, and garden at the rear where breakfast is served in the summer. Most rooms have en-suite bathrooms; apartments with kitchenettes also available. 25 rooms.

Haus International € *Elisabethstraße 87, 80797 Munich, tel: (089) 120060, fax: (089) 1200 6630, <www.hausinternational.de>.* In the heart of Schwabing, this hostel has no curfew and no age limit, and no youth hostel card is required. Includes restaurant, bar and disco. 546 beds.

Hotel Hauser € *Schellingstraße 11, 80799 Munich, tel: (089) 286 6750, fax: (089) 286 67599, <www.hotel-hauser.de>.* Small, family-run hotel garni near the University and Englischer Garten, with sauna and solarium, parking. Welcomes children. 34 rooms.

Innside Parkstadt Schwabing €€€ *Mies-van-der-Rohe-Straße 10, 80807 Munich, tel: (089) 354080, fax: (089) 3540 8299, <www.innside.de>.* Situated in the north of Schwabing (close to the motorway A9 to Nuremberg and the Mittlere Ring) this hotel at the bottom of the HighLight Towers by Helmut Jahn offers a stunning modern ambiance and utmost comfort. 160 studios and suites.

Best Western Hotel König Ludwig €€ *Hohenzollernstraße 3, 80801 Munich, tel: (089) 381520, fax: (089) 394658. <www.*

hotelkoenigludwig.de>. Hotel garni in the heart of Schwabing with comfortable rooms over seven floors. Friendly staff, serving what's claimed to be 'Munich's most lovingly-prepared breakfast'. 50 rooms.

München Marriott Hotel €€€ *Berliner Straße 93, 80805 Munich, tel: (089) 360020, fax: (089) 3600 2200, <www.marriott-muenchen.de.>*. Situated to the north of Schwabing, close to the Englischer Garten and not far from the Olympiazentrum, this hotel is known for its superb facilities, including a swimming pool, whirlpools, hydrojets, a solarium, state-of-the-art exercise equipment and saunas. 348 rooms and suites.

Mercure Schwabing €€ *Leopoldstraße 120–122, 80802 Munich, tel: (089) 389 9930, fax: (089) 349344, <www.mercure. com>*. Ideally situated hotel garni on Schwabing's main boulevard. Rooms with all mod-cons including wireless internet. 65 rooms.

München Park Hilton €€–€€€€ *Am Tucherpark 7, 80538 Munich, tel: (089) 38450, fax: (089) 3845 2588, <www.hilton.com>*. In a quiet location adjacent to the Englischer Garten, this 15-storey hotel, created for the 1972 Olympic Games, was completely renovated in 2000. Facilities include restaurant, bar, pool and fitness centre with sauna; great views of the Alps in clear weather. 479 rooms.

Hotel-Pension Am Siegestor € *Akademiestraße 5, 80799 Munich, tel: (089) 399550, fax: (089) 343050, <www.siegestor. com>*. This friendly, family-run guesthouse is spread over the top three floors of a large townhouse just 100m from the Siegestor. Some rooms with en-suite bathrooms, some shared. Great service and value. 19 rooms.

Four Points Hotel Olympiapark €€€ *Helene-Mayer-Ring 12, 80809 Munich, tel: (089) 357510, fax: (089) 3575 1800, <www. fourpoints.de/olympiapark>*. Modern hotel located in the heart of the Olympic Village, just a short walk from the Olympiapark and so ideal for those who want to make use of the facilities there. Bavarian restaurant and bar; rooms among the most modern and best kept in the city. 105 rooms.

Recommended Restaurants

This selection focuses largely on traditional Bavarian eateries and temples of gastronomy. We have included some of the major beer halls and beer gardens as they are an important focal point of Munich life; they usually serve light meals, snacks, and regional specialities. Please note that in the more expensive restaurants formal dress is expected, including a jacket and tie for men.

The following symbols correspond to the price of a 3-course meal for two people, not including wine.

€€€€	above 100 euros
€€€	75–100 euros
€€	50–75 euros
€	below 50 euros

INNENSTADT

Alois Dallmayr €€–€€€ *Dienerstraße 14–15, tel: (089) 213 5100.* Restaurant above the sumptuous delicatessen of the same name, serving superb French cuisine. Open tues–Sat 12am–2pm, 7–10pm (last order); the café is also open in the afternoon.

Zum Alten Markt €€ *Dreifaltigkeitsplatz 3, tel: (089) 299995.* Popular restaurant decorated in hunting-lodge style. The grilled meats and salads are particularly good. Reservations recommended. Open Mon–Sat 11am–midnight.

Altes Hackerhaus € *Sendlinger Straße 14, tel: (089) 260 5026.* A venerable old tavern serving typical Bavarian cuisine including calves' lung with bread dumplings and crispy roast pork knuckle with potato dumplings. Open daily 10am–midnight.

Andechser am Dom €€ *Weinstraße 7a, tel: (089) 298481.* Good-value Bavarian specialities and beer. Open daily 10–1am.

Augustiner Restaurant €€ *Neuhauser Straße 27, tel: (089) 2318 3257*. This delightful old beer hall is a Munich favourite, serving Bavarian specialities in plentiful portions. There's an attractive little garden at the back complete with fountain. Open daily.

Austernkeller €€€–€€€€ *Stollbergstraße 11, tel: (089) 298 787*. Well established seafood restaurant with the freshest oysters in town and a variety of delicious seafood selections, plus some French meat and poultry specialities. Open daily for dinner.

Böttner's €€€€ *Pfisterstraße 9, tel: (089) 221210*. A Munich institution, housed in the Renaissance Orlandohaus, with its panelled décor. Seafood specialities include lobster stew, and there is beautiful lamb and venison too. Open Mon–Sat for lunch and dinner.

Bratwurstglöckl am Dom € *Frauenplatz 9, tel: (089) 291 9450*. Old tavern serving Bavarian specialities. Known particularly for its Nürnberger Bratwurst – and the Dürer prints on the wall. Open Mon–Sat 10am–1am, Sun 11am–11pm.

Buon Gusto €€€ *Hochbrückenstraße 3, tel: (089) 296383*. Fine Italian cuisine served either in a rustic bistro or a more formal dining room, specialising in Tuscan dishes. Open Mon–Sat 11am–11pm.

Buxs €€ *Frauenstraße 9, tel: (089) 291 9550*. Self-service vegetarian restaurant offering literally dozens of dishes and salads. Food is priced by weight. Open Mon–Fri 11am–6.45pm, Sat 11am–3pm.

Ederer €€€–€€€€ *Kardinal-Faulhaberstraße 10, tel: (089) 2423 1310*. Gourmet guru Karl Ederer has established this light and airy restaurant in a former bank building in the Fünf Höfe shopping precinct. Creative interpretations of cuisines from Bavaria, France, Italy, the New World and the Pacific Rim, using seasonal produce. Open Mon–Sat for lunch and dinner.

La Galleria €€€–€€€€ *Sparkassenstraße 11, tel: (089) 297995*. Top-class Italian restaurant with excellent service and exciting, innovative cuisine. Open Mon–Sat for lunch and dinner.

Garden Restaurant €€€–€€€€ *Bayerischer Hof Hotel, Prome-nadeplatz 2–6, tel: (089) 212 0993.* Mainly Italian specialities served in style; in the garden and on the terrace of the exclusive Bayerischer Hof hotel. Open daily for lunch and dinner.

Haxnbauer €€ *Sparkassenstraße/Am Platzl, tel: (089) 216 6540.* Old Bavarian tavern specialising in spit-roast meats and regional dishes. Reservations advisable. Open daily 11am–midnight.

Hofbräuhaus am Platzl € *Am Platzl 9, tel: (089) 290 1360.* The famous Munich beer hall, in traditional Bavarian style, with live brass band music; serves sausages and regional specialities at very reasonable prices. Open daily 9am–midnight; the *Bayerische Abend* ('Bavarian Evening') of entertainment starts at 7.45pm.

Zum Hofer €€ *Burgstraße 5, tel: (089) 2421 0444.* One of the few Gothic houses left in Munich (it was once the home of the Town Clerk), with good traditional fare. In the summer, eating out in the garden is a pleasure. Open Mon–Sat 10am–1am.

Hundskugel €€ *Hotterstraße 18, tel: (089) 264272.* This inn claims to be Munich's oldest; serves good home-cooked Bavarian dishes and grilled meats in a friendly, relaxed atmosphere. Open daily 10.30am–midnight.

Kaffeehaus Dukatz in the Literaturhaus €–€€€ *Salvatorplatz 1, tel: (089) 291 9600.* One of Munich's top gathering places, with the café dedicated to the writer Oskar Maria Graf (1894–1967). The restaurant has varied and innovative French/Italian-oriented cuisine. Café open daily; restaurant closed Sunday.

Mark's €€€€ *Neuturmstraße 1, tel: (089) 2909 8875.* Munich's top luncheon venue in the luxury Mandarin Oriental hotel. Menu items change according to the season and the inspiration of the Michelin-starred chef Mario Corti. Open daily for lunch and dinner.

Mövenpick €€–€€€ *Im Künstlerhaus, Lenbachplatz 8, tel: (089) 545 9490.* A Munich favourite, with rooms devoted to different cuisines: everything from the Longhorn Corner for Texas-style steaks to Grandma's Kitchen for some old-fashioned cuisine. Kids like the Swiss *Rösti*, as well as the ice-cream. Open daily 8am–midnight.

Palaiskeller €€ *Bayerischer Hof Hotel, Promenadeplatz 2–6, tel: (089) 212 0990*. Well-prepared Bavarian cuisine in this vaulted restaurant (originally a salt store) belonging to the Bayerischer Hof Hotel, priced about the same as the beer halls and *Weinstuben* nearby. Savour the fresh pretzels from the hotel's own bakery. Open daily 10am–1am.

Prince Myschkin € *Hackenstraße 2; tel. (089) 265596*. Spacious and elegant vegetarian restaurant serving imaginative dishes ranging from Indian treats to a selection of pasta dishes and pizzas to 'classics' like the Potato-zucchini-truffle gratin. Open daily 11am–midnight.

Ratskeller €€ *Marienplatz 8, tel: (089) 219 9890*. Enormous labyrinth of an underground restaurant situated in the cellar of the Neues Rathaus. You can eat in one of the large rooms with their vaulted ceilings, or choose a more intimate booth. Typical Bavarian cuisine and plenty of beer. Open daily 10am–midnight.

Schuhbecks Südtiroler Stuben €€€€ *Am Platzl 6–8, tel: (089) 216 6900*. Acclaimed restaurant run by chef Alfons Schuhbeck, with inspired blends of Eastern and Western cuisine. Menu depends on local produce available. Open Mon–Sat for lunch and dinner.

Spatenhaus an der Oper €€–€€€ *Residenzstraße 12, tel: (089) 290 7060; <www.kuffler-gastronomie.de>*. A classic for a romantic dinner before or after visiting the opera (opposite) or one of the nearby theatres. Locals also love the cosy ground floor for morning snacks or lunches savouring Bavarian cuisine and upstairs for its more elegant atmosphere and dining.

Vinorant Alter Hof €€–€€€ *Alterhof 3, tel: (089) 2424 3733*. Excellent restaurant in the old royal palace complex serving refined versions of traditional Franconian (north Bavarian) recipes. The Hof Keller wine cellar specialises in Franconian wines and serves delicious finger foods. Open daily 11am–1am.

Weißes Bräuhaus € *Tal 7, tel: (089) 290 1380*. Rambling old Bavarian-style beer hall serving its own Schneider Weißbier (wheat beer), including the ultra-strong and dark *Aventinus*. Solid Bavarian and Austrian cuisine. Open daily 7am–midnight, longer at weekends.

Zum Spöckmeier €€ *Rosenstraße 9, tel: 268088*. This atmospheric Bavarian restaurant in the heart of Munich has been on the go since 1450. If you're there before noon, try the homemade Weißwurst, but you can drop in any time. Open daily 9am–midnight.

STATION AND THE WEST

Augustinerkeller € *Arnulfstraße 52, tel: (089) 594393*. Shady beer garden with seating for 5,000, serving *Wurst* and traditional snacks with Munich's favourite beer, Augustiner. Open daily 10am–1am.

Hirschgarten € *Hirschgartenalle 1*. Munich's largest beer garden with wonderful chestnut trees in the western district of Laim, seating 8,000, with adjoining game enclosure. Open daily 11.30am–10pm.

Löwenbräu-Keller € *Nymphenburgerstraße 2, tel: (089) 526021*. Traditional Munich beer cellar just west of the city centre, close to the museums. Open daily 9am–midnight.

Bavaria Bräu € *Theresienhöhe 7, tel: (089) 5199 7757*. In the style of a Munich beer hall serving Bavarian specialities on the outdoor terrace in summer; section for European-Asian fare and Italian dishes. Open daily 10am–midnight.

Taxisgarten € *Taxis Straße 12*. Small but very popular beer garden in the western district of Neuhausen/Gern. Open daily 11am–11pm.

ISAR AND THE EAST

Centro Español €€ *Daiserstraße. 20, tel: (089) 763653*. Small but long-established Spanish restaurant in the Sendling district, serving authentic Spanish cuisine. A variety of seafood, plus chicken and rabbit dishes and delicious *paella*. Open daily 5pm–1am.

Zum Flaucher € *Isarauen 8*. South of the centre right next to the river, this is one of Munich's best beer gardens, popular among cyclists, walkers and bathers. Open daily 10am–11pm.

Hofbräukeller €–€€ *Innere Wiener Straße 19*. Not to be confused with the Hofbräuhaus, this is a popular venue for beer garden connoisseurs in the heart of Haidhausen. Open daily 8.30am–midnight.

Käfer-Schänke €€€€ *Prinzregentenstraße 73, tel: (089) 470 6300*. Fine but casual dining in chalet-style surroundings on the upper floor of Gerd Käfer's gourmet department store near the Villa Stuck in Bogenhausen. Dishes inspired from around the world. Open Mon–Sat 11.30am–11pm.

Les Vapeurs €€€ *Regerplatz 3, tel: (089) 4444 9940*. Fabulous French cuisine in the district of Au (just south of Haidhausen), with a relaxed atmosphere and friendly, attentive service. Open Mon–Sat 6pm–1am.

Rue des Halles €€€–€€€€ *Steinstraße 18, tel: (089) 485675*. A bistro-type restaurant in Haidhausen serving quality French food, with traditional recipes rather than new creations dominating the menu. Open daily 6.30pm–1am.

Unionsbräu € *Einsteinstraße 42, tel: (089) 477677*. Situated in Haidhausen, this is of the great traditional beer cellars of Munich, with restaurant and its own small brewery. Open daily 11am–1am.

SCHWABING AND THE NORTH

Zum Aumeister € *Sondermeierstraße 9*. Favourite excursion destination on the northern edge of the English Garden, best reached by bike. 2,500 seats. Open Tues–Sun 8am–11pm.

Bamberger Haus €€–€€€ *Brunnerstraße 2, tel: (089) 308 8966*. Restaurant with lovely terrace in an 18th-century baroque villa in Luitpold Park, in the northwest of Schwabing. Traditional Bavarian food as well as international dishes. Open daily 11am–11pm.

Chinesischer Turm € *Englischer Garten 3*. One of Munich's first and largest beer gardens, in the heart of the Englischer Garten. Guests can enjoy their drinks and typical Bavarian fare to accompaniments from the live Bavarian band on the tower. 7,000 seats.

Bistro Terrine €€€€ *Amalienstraße 89 (Amalien-Passage), tel: (089) 281780*. Intimate Parisian-style restaurant in which the ingredients of classical French cuisine are combined in a modern and innovative way, changing with the seasons. The art nouveau interior is delightful, as is the peaceful terrace in the courtyard. Open Tues–Fri for lunch and dinner, Sat dinner only.

Halali €€ *Schönfeldstraße 22, tel: (089) 285909*. Traditional Munich restaurant in a baronial setting serving Bavarian dishes and also imaginative new German cuisine using local ingredients. Good service. Reservations recommended. Open Mon–Fri for lunch and dinner, Sat dinner only.

Locanda Picolit €€ *Siegfriedstraße 11, tel: (089) 396447*. Classy Italian restaurant in the heart of Schwabing, with a modern but cosy ambiance and outdoor terrace in summer on a small green square close to Münchner Freiheit. Open Sun–Fri for lunch and dinner.

Max-Emanuel-Brauerei € *Adalbertstraße 33, tel: (089) 271 5158*. Beer garden and tavern in the heart of schwabing serving typical Bavarian fare. There is live music and lively atmosphere in the hall, which is also the place to come and dance rock'n roll, salsa and the tango. Open daily 11am–1pm; beer garden to 11pm.

Osterwaldgarten €€ *Keferstraße 12, tel: (089) 3840 5040*. Renovated traditional restaurant and beer garden on the edge of the Englischer Garten, surrounded by ancient chestnut trees. Good food and excellent beer. Open daily 11am–1am.

Tantris €€€€ *Johann-Fichte-Straße 7, tel: (089) 361 9590*. Superb continental cuisine prepared by one of Germany's top chefs and served in a modern restaurant with stark and startling décor. Outdoor dining. Open Tues–Sat for lunch and dinner. Reservations essential.

INDEX